For Christians who are fee
Rahal's book is an invitati
in order to change your re
direct experiences as we
Michelle bears witness to the God in
through signs, dreams, and nudges. Michelle knows her life has been changed by these God stories and she writes to change your life as well.

—Kathy Izard, author of *The Hundred Story Home* and *The Last Ordinary Hour*

If you desire to learn more about God's mysterious ways and deepen your relationship with Him, this book is an essential guide. Saturated with surprising stories of God's unexplainable ways, *Are You Listening?* will level up your relationship with God and knowledge of the Scriptures. God is speaking all around us. May we tune our ears and heart to hear from Him in the everyday rhythms of life.

—April Dawn White, author of *Destination Hope: A Travel Companion When Life Falls Apart*

I love Michelle's heart for showing us the different ways we can hear God's voice when we listen with open hearts. It's something I've always struggled with. The stories Michelle tells about everyday people like me are a reminder to be open to the signs I might be missing in my own life. I pray it does the same for you too!

—Kim Stewart, Marketing Strategist and host of *Book Marketing Mania* podcast

For both the new Christian and the mature believer, *Are You Listening?* goes deep, challenging us to open our hearts and minds to a God who loves us enough to communicate with us regularly, personally, and often miraculously. This is so much more than simply a guide; Michelle's powerful use of storytelling, infused with relevant insights and Scripture, takes readers on a rich, compelling journey.

—Lisa Shell, CEO of *The Relatable Brand*

Are You Listening? surpasses the typical rote recitation to practice spiritual disciplines. Rahal shares contemporary examples, understandable definitions, and practical applications, all with scriptural backing. This book will equip readers to listen for and hear God's guiding voice.

—Sharon Hughson, author of *A Pondering Heart*

Are You Listening?

Are You Listening?

A Guide to Recognizing and Responding to God's Voice

Michelle Layer Rahal

Are You Listening?

Copyright© 2023 by Michelle Layer Rahal

Library of Congress Cataloging-in-Publication Data

Library of Congress Control Number: 2023911865
ISBN: 978-1-961732-02-5 (ebook)
ISBN: 978-1-961732-03-2 (paperback)

Scripture quotations marked (NIV) are taken from the Holy Bible, New International Version®, copyright © 1973, 1978, 1984, 2011 by Biblica, Inc.™ Used by permission of Zondervan. All rights reserved worldwide. The "NIV" and "New International Version" are trademarks registered in the United States Patent and Trademark Office by Biblica, Inc.™

Scripture quotations marked (NLT) are taken from the Holy Bible, New Living Translation®, copyright ©1996, 2004, 2015 by Tyndale House Foundation. Used by permission of Tyndale House Publishers, Carol Stream, Illinois 60188. All rights reserved.

Scripture quotations marked (NET) are taken from the Holy Bible, New English Translation®, copyright ©1996, 2019, used with permission from Biblical Studies Press, L.L.C. http://netbible.com. All rights reserved.

Any internet addresses (websites, blogs, etc.) in this book are offered as a resource. They are not intended in any way to be or imply an endorsement from Called Creatives Publishing, nor does Called Creatives Publishing vouch for the content of these sites for the life of this book.

All rights reserved. No portion of this book may be reproduced or shared in any form—electronic, printed, photocopied, recording, or by any information storage or retrieval system, without prior written permission from the author. The use of short quotations is permitted.

Published in association with Called Creatives Publishing,
www.calledcreativespublishing.com

Cover photo by Frasierphoto.com
Cover design: Called Creatives Publishing and Michelle Layer Rahal
Interior Formatting: Dallas Hodge

To God be the glory!
[illegible]
Eph 1:18

Dedicated to all those who don't yet recognize God's voice.

Table of Contents

Preface

Ask anyone today to tell you a story about an encounter they've had with God, and chances are you'll be met with a dumbfounded look like a deer in headlights. But ask that same person to tell you about the strangest thing they've ever experienced, something they cannot explain, and a story will often unfold in captivating detail. They might not think it's a God story they're sharing, but chances are it is if it's laced with mystery, coincidence, or bewilderment.

Ancient civilizations attributed unexplainable situations to the actions of the gods. They were attuned to the spiritual realm, which was very real to them. In today's world, however, we rely on science and logic to define the unexplainable. We attribute success to our own hard work. We write opportunities off as luck. We define chance meetings as serendipitous. Has the pendulum swung too far to the other side? Is it possible that we give logic too much credit and God too little?

Theologian and New Testament scholar John Piper tweeted in 2012, "God is always doing 10,000 things in your life, and you may be aware of three of them."[1] Such a profound statement begs the question, "If that's true, why don't we hear him all the time?" It's not because God speaks a different language; he speaks our language. And it's not because we lack the desire to hear him. We all want to hear from God. I believe it's because we are listening with the wrong ears and looking with the wrong eyes. We evaluate the world around us with our five human senses and our logical heads but rarely with our spiritual senses and surrendered hearts.

I have had the gracious honor of hearing God's audible voice several times in my life, and each time was a unique experience.

God also speaks without using language. In the absence of words, I have felt his presence, experienced his nudges, and heard him speak through others. I don't write this to boast but to testify to the mysterious proclivity God uses to communicate with each one of us in unexpected and creative ways.

That is what this book is about. Together we will look at how God has spoken to people in the past, how he speaks to people today, and how he may be trying to speak to you right now. I believe it is possible for those who desire to hear from God to do so, and I pray you are willing to try. There is an invisible world all around us waiting to be noticed and an omnipotent God waiting to be heard.

Lean into the chapters ahead, allow the stories to nurture your spiritual eyes and ears, submit to the Holy Spirit's promptings, and enjoy the journey.

Chapter 1

The Invitation: View the World Through a Divine Lens

For this people's heart has become calloused;
they hardly hear with their ears, and they have closed their eyes.
Otherwise they might see with their eyes, hear with their ears,
understand with their hearts and turn, and I would heal them.

—Matthew 13:15

With just a shovel and a hoe, I tilled and fertilized a strip of land on the side of the garage for a small vegetable garden. This was a big deal for me. Though I was raised on a modest farm in upstate New York, I was the child who preferred to stay indoors cleaning and baking. Therefore, I now had to rely on the Internet for gardening advice rather than personal experience.

Peas had to be planted weeks earlier than other seeds because they germinate better in colder weather. Zucchini needed to be planted on small mounds of dirt with plenty of space to spread out. The teeny lettuce and kale seeds would need to go in the ground next to the wall, where they would get the afternoon shade.

To my delight, every seed sprouted right on schedule, with peas and lettuce leading the way. String beans and small cucumbers came next. Later, the zucchini, squash, and tomato plants yielded yellow flowers, and I watched in hopeful expectation as blossoms turned into small vegetables. Everything was producing just as I had planned—except for the tomatoes. Though lush with leaves, the yellow blossoms had disappeared, and nothing visible had taken their place. I checked the Internet for answers but found nothing useful.

I continued to water my growing garden each morning, harvesting the vegetables that had matured and pulling up the weeds that threatened to choke them. My bushy tomato plants were filling out their cages nicely with plump green leaves, yet there was still no sign of the little red fruit. Frustrated with their performance, I barely glanced in their direction as I weeded and watered the plants around them.

The day came when I had finally had enough. If the tomato plants weren't going to be productive, they had to go so I could use the space to plant something that would produce. I marched up to those delinquent bushes and peered intently among the lush vines.

What was this? They were bursting with fruit! Each vine was blanketed with dozens of small green tomatoes that perfectly matched the color of the leaves. I had failed to notice them because I was looking for red tomatoes, like those found in the grocery store. Green tomatoes had never crossed my mind. Therefore, I could not see what I wasn't looking for.

Look Around

How often do you fail to notice what is right in front of you because your eyes are not seeking the right thing? Likewise, how often do you fail to notice God because you aren't looking for him? "He was in the world, and though the world was made through him, the world did not recognize him" (John 1:10).

I've always been perplexed as to why the synagogue leaders in Jesus' day didn't accept him as God. The Old Testament is full of prophecies that point to a suffering Messiah who would be born of a virgin in Bethlehem and ride into town on a donkey. It's not like the Jewish nation wasn't looking for the Messiah because they were. The problem was: they were looking for the wrong guy.

They expected the Messiah to arrive as a king, not as a baby. They expected him to be a conqueror, not a carpenter. They expected him to fight, not to die. Jesus did not fit the mold they had in mind. Therefore, they couldn't see him.

I'd like to claim that if I had lived in ancient Jerusalem, possessed a good understanding of the Scriptures, and witnessed miracle after miracle, I would have recognized Jesus as the Son of God. At least, that's what I'd like to think. Hindsight, however, is always 20/20.

Though Christians today declare Jesus as Lord and Savior, many forget that he is still with us, in us, and among us. He is living. He is active. He is present. The early disciples walked alongside God as Jesus in bodily form, and we get to carry the Spirit of God inside of us.

God's handiwork is everywhere. The trees and flowers. The sun and the clouds. The mountains and rivers. The birds of the air and the fish of the sea. All too often, we take these things for granted. We look at a stunning sunset and marvel at its beauty without attributing the artwork to God. We watch flowers bloom in our gardens and pat ourselves on the back for bringing them to life. We marvel at the birds that come to our feeders without a second thought as to why they appeared. "Every good and perfect gift is from above" (James 1:17). The creator of the universe is responsible for every good thing, yet we fail to give him the credit he is due. Simply put, we overlook God.

I believe there are three reasons for this. One, we are distracted by life. We become so overwhelmed with responsibilities and commitments that we fail to acknowledge the giver of life who is in the trenches with us. Two, we are rigid about our beliefs. We hold tight to the Christian principles on which we were raised and neglect to look beyond the teachings of our religious denomination for something more. Three, we are complacent. We settle for comfortable rather than extraordinary because we either fear the journey or don't want to risk losing control.

Do any of these resonate with you? Let's look at each a little closer.

One: Distracted Faith

Distractions are plentiful: family commitments, sports, entertainment, work or school, social media, personal struggles, and cultural responsibilities (just to name a few). But God is in all these things. If you want to see him, invite him to participate.

I have found that the more I acknowledge God's presence, the more I recognize when he shows up. It helps when I follow the advice of the apostle Paul to "Rejoice always, pray continually, give thanks in all circumstances; for this is God's will for you in Christ Jesus" (1 Thessalonians 5:16-18).

Rejoicing helps me turn away from anger, control, and disappointment. For example, instead of complaining when my husband leaves his shoes in the middle of the room, where I will undoubtedly trip over them, I rejoice that I have a kind and supportive husband. Rather than pointing out his flaws, I just move his shoes, and this creates a happier home for both of us. Rejoicing with a glass-half-full attitude reminds me that God is good.

Praying continually is impossible, but turning it up a notch isn't. For example, whenever I hear of someone's misfortune, pass a stranger who appears distraught, or watch a sad report unfold on the nightly news, I say a little prayer. This makes me more aware of my surroundings and invites God into the moment. And instead of saying to someone, "I will pray for you," which may or may not happen, I immediately pray over them then and there. Working prayer into opportunities as they arise reminds me that God is always present.

I'm grateful that the apostle Paul did not instruct us to give thanks *for* all circumstances but rather *in* all circumstances. An attitude of gratitude demonstrates our willingness to trust God when life seems uncertain. For example, when I suffered a stroke in my early fifties, I made it a habit to thank God for the many blessings in my life as I healed. Keeping my focus on God's promises rather than my own affliction reminded me that God had everything under control.

There is nothing you must give up to make space for rejoicing, prayer, and gratitude. Just include them in your daily distractions. Then watch how God shows up and shows off.

Two: Rigid Faith

I was raised to believe that the faith my family practiced was the "right" one. Because I knew nothing about the beliefs of any other religion or denomination, I was unable to verbalize why I believed what I believed. All I could tell you was that every other faith had it "wrong." Now that I belong to a different church than the one in which I grew up, I see that perhaps I was wrong. Some beliefs become clearer, stronger, or more authentic when we take the time to see them from a different point of view.

During the Bush-Gore presidential election of 2000, I asked my fifth-grade students to select the candidate they wanted to see win. Their homework was to watch a presidential debate on TV, read two articles about their candidate's stance on major issues, and speak to three adults who supported their choice. Along the way, they were required to take notes that would demonstrate why they supported one candidate over the other. These notes would be used at the end of the week to help them defend their choice during a classroom debate. They were stoked!

The kids came to the table prepared and passionate. There was yelling, targeted verbal attacks, name-calling, and some disrespect for the moderator—much like an actual presidential debate. After closing comments, the students cast their votes in a mock election.

Before sharing the results, I asked the question, "Did any of you change your vote based on what you heard during the debate?"

Not one hand was raised. No one had been swayed. Had they been listening?

I then instructed my students to repeat the process the following week. This time, however, they were to gather information about their rival and come to the table ready to defend the candidate they currently did not support. Silence and blank stares soon morphed into groans and anger. How could I ask them to change their stance?

I wasn't. I was merely asking them to step into someone else's shoes for a while to see things from a different perspective.

The students were wary on the day of our second debate. A week wasn't long enough for them to find their footing, and they entered the classroom with trepidation. The rules of the debate were the same as the previous week, but the students responded differently. They were quieter and more guarded. They listened to each other, offered opinions respectfully, and responded thoughtfully. They were even nicer to the moderator!

At the end of the debate, the kids cast their ballots in another mock election. Though the winner didn't change, the vote count was slightly different—enough to spark an introspective discussion. The kids noted that the second debate was calmer, which not only made them feel less agitated but also helped them focus more on the issues than the people. In addition, they recognized that each candidate had value and that neither candidate was perfect. Many of the students admitted that they had chosen to defend George W. Bush or Al Gore based on their parents' opinions, but the debate helped them realize that they could make their own decisions provided they did the proper research.

When it comes to faith, we can be as close-minded as a classroom full of fifth graders. It is not always easy to evaluate our beliefs, but it is a good first step toward tuning our ears to God's frequency.

Jesus often spoke in parables, which required his followers to pay close attention and then weigh what they heard against what they had been taught. Jesus also sparked controversy when he healed on the Sabbath, ate dinner with tax collectors, touched lepers, and overturned the money changers' tables in the courtyard of the Temple. Basically, Jesus was asking his listeners to evaluate their beliefs from a different perspective—from their hearts rather than their heads.

No matter how much we respect and appreciate what our personal church or family teaches about God, there is always more to be learned. Ask questions. Read Scripture. Visit other churches. Know what you believe and why. It is in this place of "seeking to understand" that God will speak.

Three: Complacent Faith

God never intended for us to feel satisfied in our pursuit of him. His warning to the church in Laodicea is a warning to us as well. "But since you are like lukewarm water, neither hot nor cold, I will spit you out of my mouth! You say, 'I am rich. I have everything I want. I don't need a thing!' And you don't realize that you are wretched and miserable and poor and blind and naked" (Revelation 3:16-17 NLT). In other words, we don't see what we are missing because we've settled for what we have.

Some complacent Christians don't even know they're lukewarm! I can attest to this because I was one of them. I used to go to church every Sunday, and I was content with believing that this was enough. But Jesus did not come to save me from my sins so I could give him my attention for just one hour each week. He expects and deserves more.

"Supplement your faith with a generous provision of moral excellence, and moral excellence with knowledge, and knowledge with self-control, and self-control with patient endurance, and patient endurance with godliness, and godliness with mutual affection, and mutual affection with love for everyone. The more you grow like this, the more productive and useful you will be in your knowledge of our Lord Jesus Christ" (2 Peter 1:5-8 NLT). Though God accepts us the way we are, he loves us too much to leave us that way. That's why complacency is dangerous; it hinders spiritual, intellectual, and emotional growth.

If it is your desire to see God, hear God, and recognize God in your life, you must be willing to put in the work to nurture and strengthen your faith. Eyes that truly see the Almighty and ears that truly hear his voice can be developed with practice, perseverance, and prayer.

Imagine yourself in a crowded mall where the continuous noise of shoppers melds together into one meaningless mixture of sound. Suddenly you hear a familiar voice rise above the rest. You recognize it because you know this voice well. Perhaps it belongs to your spouse or your mother. You don't need to see a face to know the speaker's identity.

In the cacophony of life, God's voice needs to become as familiar to you as a family member or a best friend. Relationships take time, effort, and commitment. But take heart! God is already a willing partner and has been calling out to you since you were born. "He will never leave you nor forsake you" (Deuteronomy 31:6).

When the Babylonians destroyed the Jerusalem temple and the people were taken into exile, they feared their connection to God had been severed as well and that they would never hear from him again. God allayed their fears through the prophet Jeremiah. "You will seek me and find me when you seek me with all your heart" (Jeremiah 29:13).

It doesn't matter who you are, where you live, or what stage of life you're in, nor do past mistakes affect future outcomes; if you seek God with your whole heart, you will come to recognize his voice. Don't settle for complacency. Seek abundance.

An Open Invitation

The first time I remember hearing God's voice was during a heated argument with my now ex-husband. He had just informed me that instead of going with me to my parents' house for Christmas, he was leaving me for another woman. And just like that, my world came crashing down. Friends and family had warned me about this man, but I didn't listen. Against their sound judgment, I accepted his invitation to move to another state, where we got married by a justice of the peace in front of strangers. Now here I was, seven years later, experiencing what they had clearly seen coming.

A tearful, angry, and confusing exchange ensued. I wanted details, explanations, and empathy, but I truly couldn't hear anything he said, nor could I make eye contact with him. I kept my head down, and I yelled. He yelled back. I cried. He clammed up. Suddenly, I heard a tender male voice say, "This is what you wanted."

My head shot up. "What does that mean?" I spewed.

My husband looked at me, confused. "I didn't say anything."

I was insistent. "Yes, you did!"

There was no denying that there had been a voice, but it hadn't come from him.

When I reflect on that moment, I know it was God speaking, telling me that I had chosen my own path. My choice of a husband was not God's choice, and it came with consequences. God would have picked someone better for me, but I never thought of asking him for guidance. I didn't know God well enough to turn to him for advice. Chalk it up to life's distractions, a rigid faith, or complacency. Whatever the reason, I knew a lot about God, but I didn't know God.

Jesus said, "My sheep listen to my voice; I know them, and they follow me" (John 10:27). God's voice was not one I recognized. Therefore, I could not follow him. Instead, I wandered off. But like a good shepherd, he came looking for me. "If a man owns a hundred sheep, and one of them wanders away, will he not leave the ninety-nine on the hills and go to look for the one that wandered off? And if he finds it, truly I tell you, he is happier about that one sheep than about the ninety-nine that did not wander off" (Matthew 18:12-13).

For much of my life, my soul had been thirsting for something greater than myself, and I had wandered off trying to quench it with the wrong things—money, hobbies, status, and my ex-husband, to name a few—false idols that couldn't gratify. After my marriage fell apart, I knew a change was necessary. I enrolled in a weekly Bible study that was held in a church unlike the one in which I had been raised. It turned out to be a passionate spiritual journey that opened my eyes and heart to a God who offered more than I could comprehend. The deeper I dove into Scripture, prayed, and practiced spiritual disciplines, the stronger my relationship with Jesus became. Author and theologian Richard J. Foster wrote, "God has given us the Disciplines of the spiritual life as a means of receiving his grace. The Disciplines allow us to place ourselves before God so that he can transform us." Transformation is necessary to become people who hear God's voice and recognize his presence.

Consider what Jesus said to the Samaritan woman at the well, "Everyone who drinks this water will be thirsty again, but whoever drinks the water I give them will never thirst. Indeed, the water I give them will become in them a spring of water welling up to eternal life" (John 4:13-14). My world had to crash before I recognized my need for a Savior.

My advice to you: Don't wait for a crash to start seeking God. He is standing by, hoping to fill your life with eternal water. You are invited to come to the well and drink deeply.

Expect the Unexpected

God will never force you to have a relationship with him. He's not demanding. Nor will he pursue you with anger or judgment if you don't seek him. He loves you and is always available to you. And because he is a creative God, he will use all sorts of methods to get your attention. But unless you become familiar with God's character, you will either not recognize his presence, or you will interpret his attempts to communicate with you as strange or coincidental.

The chapters ahead are full of wondrous stories that testify to the infinite creativity of God's interactions with humans. He makes his presence known in lights, dreams, and nature. He speaks through Scripture, strangers, and gut feelings. He answers prayers through license plates, fireflies, and closed doors. His communication tactics are extensive and cannot be anticipated.

Author Sarah Young, who excelled at the practice of hearing God, wrote down these words in her devotional book, Jesus Calling: "I speak to you continually. My nature is to communicate, though not always in words."[2] The extraordinary ways that God speaks are unfathomable, unique, and personal. It's easy to miss the signs if you aren't using your spiritual eyes and spiritual ears.

Your ability to view the world through a spiritual lens won't happen overnight—nothing extraordinary ever does. Remember, it took time and intentionality for the disciples to identify Jesus as the Son of God and to comprehend the meaning of his teachings. So, give yourself time and grace as you move slowly through this book, savoring its stories and practicing the spiritual disciplines as they are presented in the "Go Deeper" section found at the end of each chapter. As you read, examine your heart in the context of God's promises. Do not become so focused on what you expect that you lose sight of what is right in front of you.

God is calling. He wants to be a part of your life, to strengthen you and transform you, to speak to you, through you, and into you. He is not distant; he is near. Very, very near.

Are you listening?

GO DEEPER

Each morning, before my feet hit the floor, I invite the Holy Spirit to guide my steps. Sometimes I say the Lord's Prayer and meditate on the words, "Give us this day our daily bread." Sometimes I simply say, "Holy Spirit, guide my thoughts and activities this day. I don't know what is ahead, but I know you do, and I ask you to gently steer me so that all my thoughts, words, and deeds are honoring to God."

As you begin to journey through this book, I encourage you to invite the Holy Spirit into your life each day. Make up your own prayer or use a line from the Bible. Here are two that would work well: Psalm 25:4-5 states, "Show me your ways, Lord, teach me your paths. Guide me in your truth and teach me, for you are God my Savior, and my hope is in you all day long," and Psalm 143:8 reads, "Let the morning bring me word of your unfailing love, for I have put my trust in you. Show me the way I should go, for to you I entrust my life." This simple act of focusing on God first every morning will help orient your senses to the spiritual world and attune your heart to God's presence.

When you are ready, take a long, hard look at what hinders you from recognizing God's presence in your life. Are you distracted by daily tasks? Do your religious beliefs prevent you from seeing things from a different viewpoint? Are you complacent with your faith and fear trying something new? What do you need to let go of so you can grasp Jesus' hand? What is stopping you from trying? "Humble yourselves before the Lord, and he will lift you up" (James 4:10).

Journal your answers. Then rejoice, pray, and thank God for the transformation that is sure to come.

Chapter 2

Illumination: Encountering God in Light

People will tell you, "There he is!" or "Here he is!"
Do not go running off after them.
For the Son of Man in his day will be like the lightning,
which flashes and lights up the sky from one end to the other.

—Luke 17:23-24

After her first stroke, my mom walked with a limp and struggled to find the words to complete a sentence. The second stroke, which left her paralyzed on one side and unable to speak, landed her in a nursing home. The third stroke claimed her life. In many ways, Mom's passing was a relief, but that didn't make her death any easier to accept.

Family and friends gathered for the funeral in upstate New York to offer their condolences for the woman I had the privilege to call "Mom." I was grateful that snow hadn't ruined the occasion, which is always a strong possibility in January. Tears mingled with laughter as we reminisced about her homemade pies, gorgeous quilts, and distinctive squeals that erupted whenever she lost a bid during a card game.

I promised my grieving father that I would visit him in a month, and cousins who attended the funeral offered to check in on him. My siblings and I discussed plans to get our families together for the summer. But none of this was to be. Days after the funeral, the Coronavirus started shutting down the world.

It was a cold February evening when my husband and I headed to our hot tub to reflect on all that had occurred over the last several weeks. Though grateful for the time we had spent with family and friends, we couldn't help but wonder how long it would be before another family reunion was possible. Would we have to spend Easter alone? Could we bring my father to our house for a long stay? When would we see our siblings again?

As the warm water bubbled around us beneath a clear Virginia sky, a flash of bright light suddenly enveloped us. My husband and I yelped in shock before the light disappeared completely. Greg, the level-headed engineer, searched for an explanation. "Was that lightning?"

"I think we'd be dead if it were," I answered. After all, we were perched like lightning rods in a big tub of water.

"Do you think someone just snapped our picture?" was his next question.

Seeing as we live on an acre of land in a relatively wooded area, it seemed improbable that someone had just come into our yard, snapped a picture, and run off without us hearing or seeing a thing. Besides, the flash of a camera would have come from a horizontal level, which was not the case. This light had come out of nowhere.

"No. No one took our picture," I answered.

"Aliens?" he smirked.

I smiled. "I don't think so."

Greg and I discussed the facts. The light was bright and enveloping. It was not accompanied by any sound, and the intensity of the flash did not affect the electric lights on our deck or in the hot tub itself. Since we could not come to a logical conclusion for the sudden illumination, we settled on the supernatural. We had experienced a holy moment like the one reflected in Psalm 29:7. "The voice of the Lord strikes with flashes of lightning." God had spoken, but not with words.

When faced with situations we don't understand, we humans want practical answers. But God doesn't work that way. He operates in the unexplainable margins of our logical lives. He is a God of surprises.

The Goodness of Light

In the beginning, the Bible tells us the earth was formless, empty, and dark. "And God said, 'Let there be light,' and there was light" (Genesis 1:3). There are two things worth noting here. The first is that the darkness existed before the light, when the earth was formless and empty. Creation began when God spoke the light into existence and declared it was good. God did not necessarily create darkness; all we know is that it was present in the beginning.

The second thing to note is that Jesus is the light and was, therefore, present at creation. The apostle John wrote, "The Word gave life to everything that was created, and his life brought light to everyone. The light shines in the darkness, and the darkness can never extinguish it" (John 1:4-5 NLT). Think about that. It is not possible for the dark to extinguish the light because darkness has no value or power of its own. When we enter a dark room, we can turn the light on, but we cannot turn the darkness off. Only God can do that through the Son.

The absence of light can be frightening. When our visual senses are compromised, we imagine terrible scenarios. God capitalized on this when he plunged Egypt into total darkness for three days. "The Lord said to Moses, 'Extend your hand toward heaven so that there may be darkness over the land of Egypt, a darkness so thick it can be felt'" (Exodus 10:21 NET). This sentence gives me pause. Is it even possible to feel darkness? Maybe not with our human senses, but surely with our spiritual senses. When God plunged Egypt into a darkness so thick it could be felt, he not only removed the Egyptians' ability to see, he also removed himself from their presence. In the absence of God, evil can be felt.

The Israelites, too, encountered darkness when they followed Moses out of Egypt into the wilderness. But they had nothing to fear because God was always before them, guiding their steps. "Neither the pillar of cloud by day nor the pillar of fire by night left its place in front of the people" (Exodus 13:22).

Another provision of light is life itself. I remember a second-grade science project my teacher assigned on the importance of sunlight. Each student was given two small Dixie cups and two dried peas. We were instructed to plant a pea in each cup using soil from our backyards. One of the cups was to be placed on a sunny windowsill and the other in a dark cupboard. Each day we had to water our seeds and record what we saw.

The seed in the cup on the windowsill sprouted within a week. After two weeks, it was over an inch tall. But the Dixie cup in the cupboard showed no signs of life, except for a little mold, which only worsened during week three.

Like plants, humans cannot thrive without light. There's even a disease that brings on feelings of depression caused by a decrease in sunlight. It's called SAD, which stands for Seasonal Affective Disorder. Sunlight is good for our health on several levels. Studies show it improves sleep quality, reduces high blood pressure, and helps regulate our immune systems.

Our physical bodies need light to thrive, but our souls need Jesus, the light of the world, to survive.

The Light of Christ

Jesus said, "I am the light of the world. Whoever follows me will never walk in darkness but will have the light of life" (John 8:12). Because God wants us to choose eternal life (light) over spiritual death (darkness), he will resort to drastic measures to get our attention when necessary.

Phil was the son of a Methodist pastor. He had grown up in the church, was an active member in the youth program, and thought he knew the message of the gospel, but he didn't believe all he had heard. Phil did not acknowledge the virgin birth, the resurrection, or the Biblical stories of most miracles. So, when a congregant asked Phil, "Are you going to follow in your dad's footsteps?" he replied with ease, "My beliefs are not compatible with his profession."

At age seventeen, Phil signed up with a secular international student exchange program. He was excited to learn that he had been assigned to live with a family in Alsace, France for the summer. He was less enthusiastic about his work assignment, which was picking cherries for ten hours a day, six days a week, on the family's fruit farm. To make matters worse, his French "brother" was a born-again Christian who took every opportunity to challenge Phil about his faith. Phil listened respectfully but was not swayed by anything his French brother said about God.

After two months of committed labor, Phil managed to negotiate for a day off. Having no friends other than his fellow cherry pickers, his only plan was to sleep in, tucked away in the small room he had all to himself. To prevent any sunlight from disrupting his plan, Phil closed the wooden shutters tightly over the lone window before going to bed.

When Phil woke the next morning, he noticed a bright point of light seeping through a very small hole in the shutters on the opposite wall. As he stared, the light grew more intense. Soon it surrounded him until it filled the entire room. Phil felt a flush of inner warmth, which he described as a feeling of elation mixed with a little fear. In Phil's words, "The room wasn't just illuminated; it was total light, and I was enveloped in it. All I could think was, 'It's Jesus.'"

But then doubt crept in. Instantly, faster than the blink of an eye, the brilliant light was reduced to a dim ray of morning sun leaking through the slats of the shutters. Phil found himself in near-total darkness, contemplating what had just happened.

The great evangelist John Wesley, who initiated the Methodist movement, once described the feeling of being in God's presence as having his "heart strangely warmed."[3] This, too, is how Phil described his experience in that illuminated bedroom in Alsace. "For just a few seconds," he says, "I felt like I was in the presence of God—until I tried to rationalize the experience."

Phil's life didn't change that day. He still resisted faith, but he often wondered if there was more. Experiencing God as the light of the world that day in France was the spark that made Phil receptive to the Holy Spirit's flame. Several months later, Phil made a conscious decision to follow Christ. Then years later, during a time of meditation that turned into prayer, Phil experienced a sense of elevation that completely opened his heart to God.

Looking back, Phil admits that God pursued him like a hunting dog but gave him enough time and space to come to his own conclusions. Today Phil admits that it was probably Jesus who visited him in Alsace, and he acknowledges that his life would be very different had he dismissed the light as anything less than divine.

Phil's experience with the Light of the World was patient and gentle—quite different from the dramatic encounter Saul experienced on the road to Damascus.

After Jesus' death and resurrection, Saul went on a mission to persecute the followers of Jesus. With special permission from the high priest in Jerusalem, Saul headed north to seek and destroy any followers of "The Way" who had infiltrated the synagogues there. "As he neared Damascus on his journey, suddenly a light from heaven flashed around him. He fell to the ground and heard a voice say to him, 'Saul, Saul, why do you persecute me?'" (Acts 9:3-4).

Double whammy! Light *and* the voice of God!

Saul's response—falling to his knees when the light flashed around him—demonstrates his recognition of the supernatural. He didn't pull out a knife to defend himself from a possible attack; he fell to his knees in submission. I can only imagine the shock Saul felt when he inquired of the light's identity and heard, "I am Jesus, whom you are persecuting. Now get up and go into the city, and you will be told what you must do" (Acts 9:5-6).

It wasn't until Saul stood and opened his eyes that he discovered he was unable to see. Saul alone was blinded by the light; his traveling companions were not. God showed up in full force for one person only.

For three days, Saul fasted in total darkness, utterly dependent on God's grace. He must have wondered if this was his eternal fate or if the Lord would one day free him from blindness. The fact that he fasted tells us that Saul was in anguish, either unable to eat because of the severity of his situation or unwilling to eat in repentance for his sin of persecuting Christians. I believe God allowed Saul to sit in darkness for several reasons. One, he would come to understand what the world would feel like without the light of Christ. Two, it made him obedient to God's will. Three, it forced him to look at life with his heart.

On the third day, a man who was obedient to God's call came to the house where Saul was fasting and, laying his hands on him, restored his sight. Once his eyes were opened, Paul (as he was now called) began to preach about Jesus as the light of Christ, literally and figuratively. In so doing, Paul did more for the advancement of Christianity than perhaps any of the other apostles.

Light Comes in Many Sizes

My husband and I were flashed with light. Phil was enveloped in light. Paul was blinded by light. And Minh Phuong, a Vietnamese refugee, was touched by light. Having faced death multiple times, she was keenly aware of God's saving grace; however, she had never experienced God as light. That changed during her third year in seminary.

Having not yet mastered the English language, Minh found her grades sinking in Hebrew and Greek. Far away from the support of family and friends who had either died or lived halfway across the world, she began to question her abilities and worth. In her memoir, *Straining Forward*, Minh tells how she went on a long walk with God one evening to find the strength to carry on in her loneliness. God responded with the appearance of hundreds of fireflies.

> I watched in amazement as each insect's light came to life for only a few seconds before another took its place. It was like a well-synchronized dance or a well-rehearsed symphony of light—and I was the lone audience member. My heart rejoiced at the performance.
>
> As I stood watching the fireflies appear and disappear, I was reminded of all the people I had known whose presence in my life had been short-lived. They were all flickers of light in my otherwise dark world. Here today and gone tomorrow, evidence of God's blessings and enduring faithfulness.[4]

Minh's encounter with the fireflies was a gentle indication that she was not alone; God was with her. Those small flickers of light gave her the encouragement she needed to keep studying and not doubt her call to ministry. Minh went on to complete her studies and became the third Asian woman in America to be ordained a Presbyterian pastor.

God's light can appear in any form, any size, and at any time. So, keep your eyes open for the kind of light that speaks to your heart. "We know that the world in its current state, without the help of Jesus, is dark. God doesn't have to add his power to crush what is already headed for destruction, but he is asking us to partner with redemption, transformation, and hope."[5]

This brings me full circle to the experience my husband and I had in our hot tub. Our discussion centered on fear associated with the pandemic. On top of grieving my mother's death, I was also lamenting the loss of normalcy in the world. That unexplainable flash of light brought our mournful discussion to an immediate end. I believe it was God's way of saying, "I have everything under control. Stop worrying."

I consider it a blessing of great significance that God allowed my husband and me to experience that holy moment together. In both the Old and New Testaments, Scripture stresses the importance of the testimony of two or three witnesses. "One witness is not enough to convict anyone accused of any crime or offense they may have committed. A matter must be established by the testimony of two or three witnesses" (Deuteronomy 19:15). I don't know when God might call Greg or me forward to testify to his active presence in our lives, but when he does, we will be able to back each other up.

Not every flash of light or cluster of fireflies is a message from God, but if you are wrestling with an issue or have been praying for direction, pay close attention to the illumination that mysteriously appears when you least expect it. If the light is from God, it will contain a message that was scripted specifically for you. Don't write it off as unexplainable. There is an explanation: God is speaking.

GO DEEPER

Many ancient cultures worshipped the sun as God, but today we Christians know that the sun is a ball of hot plasma. It was created by God when "he separated the light from the darkness" (Genesis 1:4). The sun, in all its glory, radiates God's magnificence, and a sunrise reminds us of his promised return.

Pick a day that you can wake up early to experience the rising sun, and select a spot with a clear view of the eastern horizon. Ideally, you should plan to sit quietly in the dark for approximately 30 minutes before the sun rises.

Once you have settled in, pray in the darkness. Share your worries and concerns with God. Tell him your hopes and dreams. Acknowledge and confess your sins. "If we confess our sins, he is faithful and just and will forgive us our sins and purify us from all unrighteousness" (1 John 1:9). Then sit back and let the sun rise upon you. As a new day ushers in, relinquish your cares to God and accept his warm, cleansing light.

Do not rush this time with the creator. Notice the beauty in the colors of the sunrise. Take note of how your surroundings come into view. Pay attention to your feelings. Praise God for who he is, and thank him for all the lights in your life.

Take this experience into your day and use it to illuminate the lives of the people you encounter. During the Sermon on the Mount, Jesus told the crowd, "You are the light of the world. A town built on a hill cannot be hidden. Neither do people light a lamp and put it under a bowl. Instead, they put it on a stand, and it gives light to everyone in the house" (Matthew 5:14-15).

Pay attention to your words and actions. Smile more. Move slowly and with intention. Let your words be uplifting and encouraging.

A new day dawns every morning. Do not take this gift for granted. May it serve as a reminder that God is with you, guiding and protecting you. Rest in the knowledge that you are a child of the light and no longer walk in darkness.

Chapter 3

Dreams and Visions: The Invisible Becomes Visible

And afterward, I will pour out my Spirit on all people.
Your sons and daughters will prophesy,
your old men will dream dreams, your young men will see visions.

—Joel 2:28

The email from David was addressed to "Dear beloved friends." Because I had been blind copied, I didn't know who else had received the letter. I kept reading.

> A couple of nights ago, I had a bizarre and somewhat troubling dream. In the dream, I was speaking with a couple of prominent national politicians (with whom I have never had a conversation) when I was introduced to an older gentleman (again, someone I did not know) who implored me to reach out to an old friend of mine who was deeply troubled and mentally exhausted. In short, he was on the verge of suicide. He asked whether I could check in on him. You can only imagine that I awoke in a panic. The person that was identified [in the dream] is fine, but what I've learned from my dreams is that often a person that has been shown in my dreams is just a representation of someone else who may be the real subject, which is the reason for my note to all of you.

I had known David for several years, but until I received this note, I was unaware of his rich dream life. His email was an invitation for me to learn more about how God speaks through dreams today.

Follow the Dream

Humans have been fascinated by dreams for much of recorded history. The ancient Egyptians believed that the gods communicated directly with humans while they slept. Mesopotamians and Greeks, in search of divine advice, would sleep in the presence of their idols in a special room within a temple. Many Native American cultures consider the dream space to be sacred, a place where nature speaks to man. For Australian Aborigines, dreamtime is the pathway to connect with ancestral spirits. It wasn't until the nineteenth century that the interpretation of dreams turned away from the supernatural and toward man's deepest self. Both Sigmund Freud and Carl Jung speculated that dreams provide insight into the inner workings of the complex mind.[6]

While today's neuroscientists may disagree on their purpose, there is no denying that dreams have provided certain individuals with prophetic messages, visits from loved ones, warnings, and solutions. Therefore, whether dreams stem from the supernatural world or the subconscious mind, it does not alter God's power over them. Dreams are yet another communication tool in God's utility bag. "For God speaks, the first time in one way, the second time in another, though a person does not perceive it. In a dream, a night vision, when deep sleep falls on people as they slumber in their beds" (Job 33:14-15 NET).

Omoanghe Isikhuemhen is a microbiologist from Nigeria, which is where he got his start in the field of mushrooms. He furthered his studies and research in Germany, Prague, Japan, and the United States and went on to become one of the world's leading mushroom experts. Since 2002, Isikhuemhen has been working on cultivating truffles in North Carolina. These prized mushrooms are not typically cultivated but rather foraged. Previous attempts at "truffle farming has been a 20-year train wreck."[7] But that is changing under Isikhuemhen's expertise. When a Smithsonian reporter asked the scientist how he came up with the mix that would grow truffles five times faster than ever before, he answered, "It came to me in a dream." Isikhuemhen added, "When you get such messages from the divine, you work with them."

Ancient cultures were better at this than society today. They expected their dreams to provide direction while we barely acknowledge their potential.

In the first book of the Bible, God uses a dream to issue a big warning to Abimelech, the king of Gerar. Fearing death, Abraham lies to Abimelech about Sarah's true identity as his wife. Abimelech then takes Sarah, whom he believes to be Abraham's sister, into his house to have his way with her. But before Abimelech lays a hand on Sarah, God appears to him in a dream and says, "You are as good as dead because of the woman you have taken, for she is someone else's wife!" (Genesis 20:3 NET). Abimelech pleads with God not to punish him for Abraham's deception, and God complies.

The important thing to take from this encounter is that Abimelech did not ignore the dream or write it off as a reflection of his subconscious mind. He paid attention. He heeded God's message. By so doing, he saved his own skin and kept Sarah's reputation intact.

My friend David responded similarly. Experience had taught him to pay attention to his dreams—particularly the message, not necessarily the people.

David is a former Capitol Hill lobbyist, so it's no surprise that he dreamt of chatting with two prominent female members of Congress. Though he'd never met either of these women in real life, they were a part of his subconscious mind. The wise, older gentleman, however, was not someone David had ever seen before. He gave David an explicit direction. "You really need to check in on our mutual friend, Alex. We are really worried about him."

Upon waking, David immediately made the call. He didn't wait or put it off. He acted.

Alex answered the phone from a hospital where he was recovering from surgery. David was able to pray with his friend and encourage him in his recuperation. Truly a bonus blessing, David admitted, but not a fulfillment of the dream's directive.

The clock was ticking, and David felt it. Unsure of whom to reach out to next, he wrote an email that he blind-copied to about forty friends. He also posted that same note on Facebook, which had the potential to reach hundreds of people. Within minutes, one person responded. Just one. The right one.

"If I hadn't seen your email," she wrote, "I don't know what I would have done."

I asked David to speculate on what he thought might have happened had he not acted quickly on his dream. Though he could only guess, he assured me that any other scenario just wasn't an option. Years of hearing from God through his dreams had taught David to pay attention and act quickly.

David's dream life has gotten stronger and richer over the years as his relationship with God deepened. David says, "God uses dreams to say to me, 'Hey, this is just a taste of what we could be engaged in!'"

Heed the Warnings

God does not need us to carry out his plans. Rather, he invites us to participate in them. If we ignore or fail to act on an invitation we receive in a dream, we do so at our own peril. Consider the story of Pilate's wife.

The chief priests had no authority to kill Jesus, so they brought him before Pilate, the governor of Judea, for sentencing. Pilate questioned Jesus but found no reason to condemn him to death.

"While Pilate was sitting on the judge's seat, his wife sent him this message: 'Don't have anything to do with that innocent man, for I have suffered a great deal today in a dream because of him'" (Matthew 27:19). Instead of honoring his wife's request, Pilate asked the crowd for their opinion on what to do with Jesus. With the chief priests and elders urging them on, the crowd yelled, "Crucify him!"

"When Pilate saw that he was getting nowhere, but that instead an uproar was starting, he took water and washed his hands in front of the crowd. 'I am innocent of this man's blood,' he said" (Matthew 27:24). Not only did Pilate refuse to heed the warning from his wife's dream, but he also refused to take responsibility for his actions.

As Christians, we understand that Jesus had to die for our sins—that's the reason he came to earth in human form. But is it possible that someone other than Pilate was supposed to pronounce the death sentence? Unlike Abimelech, who heeded his dream and was spared, Pilate ignored the dream he was given and suffered for it. Though there are conflicting stories about what became of Pilate after the crucifixion, most are not good. Unless he retired into obscurity, he was either executed by Emperor Caligula, sent into exile where he committed suicide, or became a Christian and was martyred. Whatever his demise, one thing is certain: Ignoring a God-given dream has its consequences.

Dreams from Heaven are Memorable

Not all dreams are messages from God. Those who experience divine dreams, however, describe them as hyper-real, intense, emotional, long-lasting, and life-changing.

As a young man, Thomas was somewhat of a prankster and rebel. Everyone expected a good laugh whenever they were in his presence. Thomas also possessed a competitive mindset and pushed himself harder than most people. When he was a sophomore in college, he suffered a terrible mountain climbing accident that plunged him into a coma for several weeks. The night after he woke up, he experienced a vivid dream.

In his dream, Thomas was walking along a lakeshore and came upon a boathouse. The inside was arrayed with a collection of beautiful eight-person crew shells—a type of racing boat measuring about 55 feet in length. Shells today are generally constructed of fiberglass or light carbon fiber, but the shells Thomas saw were made of wood. One old wooden shell was not on the rack but rather resting in maintenance slings, where an older man gently worked the hull with a little piece of fine sandpaper. The tenderness with which the rigger rubbed the boat made the woodgrain pop. Thomas was flabbergasted by its beauty and said to the man, "This is incredible!"

The man smiled and said, "You should see what's outside."

Thomas exited the boathouse by way of the dock. Once outside, he realized he was flying, and all around him were big, beautiful, ancient galleons. Each had been hand-sanded and stained till it sparkled like the sun. Instinctively, Thomas knew that each boat was loved deeply and had been patiently refined for God's kingdom purposes.

Dreams are individual experiences, and every dream is open to interpretation, but the message Thomas received serves as a message for all of us who hear it. God hand-sands each of us individually. He patiently takes off our rough edges with sandpaper. Though it may hurt a little, God is with us, turning us into the beautiful vessels he intended for us to be.

Many of us cannot remember our dreams upon waking, and some of us aren't even sure that we dreamed at all. (I fall into that category.) But those who do receive a message from God in their dreams are able to share vivid details that do not appear to fade or change over time.

The Gift of Visions

Unlike dreams, which occur during sleep, visions occur during times of consciousness. People who experience visions see things in the present that others do not. A clear illustration of this can be found in the Old Testament, where the Arameans are warring with the Israelites. Every attempt made by the king of Aram to infiltrate Israel is met with defeat. Enraged, the king calls in his officers and demands to know who is leaking information to his opponent. "'It's not us, my lord and king,' one of the officers replied. 'Elisha, the prophet in Israel, tells the king of Israel even the words you speak in the privacy of your bedroom'" (2 Kings 6:12 NLT). Talk about being a fly on the wall!

The king of Aram, knowing he cannot succeed as long as the prophet is alive, orders an army to capture Elisha.

> When the servant of the man of God got up early the next morning and went outside, there were troops, horses, and chariots everywhere. "Oh, sir, what will we do now?" the young man cried to Elisha.
>
> "Don't be afraid," Elisha told him. "For there are more on our side than on theirs."
>
> Then Elisha prayed, "O Lord, open his eyes and let him see!" The Lord opened the young man's eyes, and when he looked up, he saw that the hillside around Elisha was filled with horses and chariots of fire. (2 Kings 6:15-17 NLT)

Can you imagine? One minute you're shaking in your boots as you stare down at an invading army, and the next minute you see that you are surrounded by heavenly horses and chariots of fire in your defense. What a sensation to witness God's army fighting our battles!

Those who experience visions today claim to see the kingdom of God in the here and now. Lira is one of those people for whom the invisible becomes visible. In her teens, she started experiencing vivid dreams. Later in life, she prayed in earnest that God would open her eyes and ears to his will. Specifically, Lira requested the gift of prophecy. As an artist and designer, she felt her relationship with God would blossom best if the Lord communicated with her visually.

She prayed. She fasted. She meditated. "Call to me and I will answer you and tell you great and unsearchable things you do not know" (Jeremiah 33:3). As Lira focused her whole desire on God's will through the gift of visions, the spiritual realm opened to her. She saw heaven and its angels as well as hell and its demons. "I can see a whole divine movie in front of me," Lira says. She compares it to looking through a windshield. You can either look through the glass to see what's out there, or you can look at the glass and see the bugs. When Lira has a vision, she sees both views—the present and the divine—at the same time.

One important thing God revealed to Lira was that spiritual warfare is as real now as it was in Elisha's day, and humans possess the greatest weapon in the fight: praise. Singing is ammunition, and dancing is serious weaponry. King David may have known this when he ushered the Ark of the Covenant into Jerusalem. "Wearing a linen ephod, David was dancing before the Lord with all his might, while he and all Israel were bringing up the ark of the Lord with shouts and the sound of trumpets" (2 Samuel 6:14).

Imagine the gains we could make in the spiritual realm if we all regularly danced and sang as King David did. As Christians, every action we take has the power to advance the kingdom of God here on earth. Every call to action we ignore gives the enemy an advantage.

Several years after acquiring the gift of visions, Lira attended a Fellowship of Christian Athletes event where my dear friend, Shontya, was the guest speaker. During the event, Lira felt God urging her to pray for Shontya, and that prayer turned into a vision. Afterward, Lira approached my friend to share what she had seen.

Shontya was heading into a battle of some sort, riding on a white horse flanked by angels that were either blowing huge trumpets or beating on drums. Lira told Shontya not to lose heart because the angels were cheering her on.

What Lira didn't know was that Shontya was about to throw her hat into the ring for political office. The campaign was going to be tough and dirty because she was the lone black candidate among a field of older, white men in a confederate-minded area of Virginia. The message Lira carried to Shontya encouraged her and provided the confidence she needed to stay the course.

Visions make one thing very clear: we are not in control. However, we can align ourselves with the One who is.

God as Interpreter

Spiritual dreams and visions can be confusing or illogical to our human mind. Since God alone initiates them, he alone can interpret them. Therefore, if God gives you a dream or vision that does not make sense, turn to him for clarity.

Authors Adam F. Thompson and Adrian Beale offer helpful advice. "Start by asking Holy Spirit to help you understand what is being communicated in the event. Next, identify the elements that make up the scene, being sensitive to any related passages of Scripture that come to mind."[8] Then pray that God will expand your understanding and reveal the purpose of what you saw. Meditate on the dream or vision to obtain clarity. Then act as you feel God is calling you to do, even if it seems strange or contrary to your own beliefs.

Dreams and visions are beneficial to each of us because they reveal God's glory and strengthen our relationship with the Lord when we act on them. When we ignore these divine messages, however, they expose our fallibility and allow the enemy to move forward. We may not see what is happening in the spiritual realm, but God does, and he lovingly invites us to participate in the battle with him.

GO DEEPER

Author C.S. Lewis wrote, "As long as you are proud, you cannot know God."[9] And if you do not know God, you cannot recognize when he is speaking to you in your dreams. Pride is a self-conscious emotion that hinders us from praising God with every fiber of our being. Instead of dancing and singing with abandon, as King David did in 2 Samuel chapter 6, we hold back or pander to the public, as Pilate did in Matthew chapter 27. In so doing, we limit our ability to hear and see God.

Try letting your defenses down. Search the Internet for "contemporary Christian dance music" to find a song you like. Then blast it on your speakers, close your eyes, and dance before the Lord. If this is too much of a stretch for you, start with whatever music you are comfortable with. The point is to let go and let your body praise God. "Do not be afraid of those who kill the body but cannot kill the soul. Rather, be afraid of the One who can destroy both soul and body in hell" (Matthew 10:28). Don't worry about what you look like. God is your only audience, and he is looking at your heart.

Before going to bed, ask God to speak to you in your dreams. You might want to keep a pad of paper and pen by the bed to take notes in the dark. If you do experience a vivid dream, take time to pray about it in the morning and ask God to make its interpretation clear. It goes without saying that directives from God are to be carried out faithfully, but make sure the message aligns with God's character. God will never ask you to harm or mislead another person.

Therefore, if God's goodness is not recognizable in your dream, ask him to give you the wisdom to understand what he is saying. "If any of you lacks wisdom, you should ask God, who gives generously to all without finding fault, and it will be given to you" (James 1:5).

Chapter 4

Spiritual Intuition: Attending to Gut Feelings

For wisdom will enter your heart,
and knowledge will be pleasant to your soul.
Discretion will protect you, and understanding will guard you.

—Proverbs 2:10-11

Jerry is a soft-spoken man with gray hair and gentle eyes. You would never know by looking at him that he was once a drug addict and alcoholic. He started using when he was in middle school, and by the time he turned 20, Jerry was selling drugs to pay for his habit. It wasn't until he was facing eviction and possible arrest that Jerry admitted to himself that he had a problem. Hoping to turn his life around, Jerry booked a room in a residential detox center.

The day before his lock-in, Jerry decided to get rid of all the drugs and alcohol in his possession by binging. He smoked two joints, drank five beers, and then headed to his friend's place to finish off the rest of his "crank," which is slang for Methamphetamine. Several drug users were at the house when Jerry arrived, so there was plenty of dope to go around. But what Jerry really wanted was a cigarette, and there weren't any. The corner store was only a couple of blocks away, so he headed out for a pack of Marlboros.

Jerry's walk was briefly interrupted when he heard music coming from a small church he had never noticed before. The song sounded familiar, and he slowed his pace to listen. But when the song ended, Jerry made a beeline to the store. He might have succeeded in getting totally wasted that night if not for the music he heard on his way back. Something about the melody stopped him in his tracks and made him think, "Perhaps God can break my addiction."

Thinking it rude to enter a church with cigarettes, Jerry ran to his friend's house and dropped them off. Then he quickly headed back to the church. Even without the Marlboros, Jerry must have been a sight to behold. He was wearing ripped jeans and a T-shirt with a torn pocket; he hadn't shaved in several days and was high on marijuana. Ashamed and hoping to go unnoticed, Jerry sat in the very last pew. But no sooner did he take a seat when the pastor called on the woman sitting directly in front of him to stand and give her testimony. All eyes turned to look at the woman but landed on the stranger behind her.

The woman's testimony was unlike anything Jerry had ever heard. It was a strip-and-grip story: God strips away everything you hold dear, and you grip God as your Savior. A severe car accident had placed this woman in a body brace. She relied on friends, weekly injections, and painkillers to get her through each day. Broken and suffering, she decided to take her life. But as she lifted a hand of pills to her mouth to overdose, she felt the Holy Spirit come over her, push her hand away, and replace her pain with a sense of peace.

Jerry was captivated. He understood addiction; he understood emotional pain. He knew what it was like to lose control of his life and to be disappointed in himself. But Jerry couldn't make sense of the Holy Spirit experience.

At that very moment, Jerry felt a warm wave of acceptance come over him. It was calming and kind. He knew immediately and, without a shadow of a doubt, that it was the same Holy Spirit that had blessed the woman in front of him. Jerry started sobbing uncontrollably as a gentle force pulled him out of his seat and walked him down the center aisle toward the altar.

The Call of the Spirit

Have you ever experienced a gut feeling, a hunch, or an intuition? In some cases, it's human instinct. In others, it's the call of the Holy Spirit.

Though both human instinct and spiritual intuition call us to act independently of any reasoning process, they are quite different. Human instinct derives from the subconscious mind to alert us to danger without the support of conscious intellect. It usually elicits a physical response, like a sick feeling in the stomach or heavy breathing. Spiritual intuition, on the other hand, goes beyond our physical senses. Because the feeling is not driven by our own subconscious but rather by the Holy Spirit within, the corresponding feeling is usually one of peace, acceptance, and love. Unlike human instinct that says, "run," spiritual intuition says, "stay."

Luke, in the book of the Bible that bears his name, relays the story of two people who encounter Jesus after his resurrection as they walked to Emmaus, "but they were kept from recognizing him" (Luke 24:16). Jesus and the other two travelers arrived in the village as night was beginning to fall. In the ancient tradition of hospitality, the two people urged Jesus to stay. "When [Jesus] was at the table with them, he took bread, gave thanks, broke it, and began to give it to them. Then their eyes were opened and they recognized him, and he disappeared from their sight. They asked each other, 'Were not our hearts burning within us while he talked with us on the road and opened the Scriptures to us?'" (Luke 24:30-32).

Their hearts were burning—not in pain, but in pleasure. They felt a joy that compelled them to invite their traveling companion to stay with them for the night. This was a Holy Spirit moment: delightful and fulfilling, one that left the recipients feeling wholly content and lovingly transformed.

Transformation Through the Spirit

Jerry couldn't recall how long he lay on the ground in front of the altar weeping, but when he gained control of himself, he ran—down the center aisle, out the same door he had entered, and back to his friend's place where things were predictable. But they weren't.

Jerry found his tribe zoned out in front of the television, incapable of acknowledging his presence. Grabbing the pack of cigarettes from the coffee table where they had hurriedly been discarded, Jerry tapped one out and put it between his lips. He was used to smoking two packs a day, but now he discovered that he had no desire to light up. Dumbfounded, Jerry decided to calm his nerves with the two joints hidden in the glove compartment of his car. They were easy enough to find but harder to light because Jerry had no desire to smoke them. He had the same adverse reaction when he popped open a can of beer.

"What is going on?" Jerry wondered. "What has happened to me?" Confused and feeling strangely sober, Jerry threw the pack of cigarettes into the trash can and headed home.

When the alarm went off at 7:00 a.m., Jerry awakened from one of the sweetest nights of sleep he could ever remember. His soul felt at peace, his heart was joyful, and his body was not experiencing any symptoms of a hangover. Jerry pulled himself out of bed and began to look around his bedroom in awe. Everything was glistening, as if it was glowing from within. "This means that anyone who belongs to Christ has become a new person. The old is gone; a new life has begun!" (2 Corinthians 5:17 NLT). Jerry walked slowly from one room to another, trying to make sense of it all. Things looked different. Things *were* different. Life was different. He was different.

At the core of his being, Jerry felt these words: "Don't go." The words were not audible per se, yet they resonated in his very soul as if he was hearing them through his heart. The feeling only got stronger as he began packing for the detox program.

"Don't go."

Pushing the intuition aside, Jerry threw a few more things into his suitcase.

"Don't go."

The Holy Spirit was offering Jerry an opportunity to break free of addiction without human help. It was unfathomable but impossible to ignore. Jerry acknowledged the silent whisper and accepted the offer. Instead of heading to rehab that morning, he returned to the church that night and the next and every night of that two-week revival. His addiction to drugs, alcohol, and cigarettes was completely obliterated, replaced by a desire for more of God and the Holy Spirit.

"You, my brothers and sisters, were called to be free. But do not use your freedom to indulge the flesh; rather, serve one another humbly in love" (Galatians 5:13). As Jerry found his spiritual footing, his personal life took on meaning. He enrolled in college, got a degree in psychology, and eventually obtained licenses to counsel in four areas of substance abuse. God brought Jerry full circle when he placed him in a shelter working with street people, in prison with drug addicts, and in a halfway house running a methadone clinic. Though Jerry never checked into that detox center as a patient, he did end up working there later in life.

God turned Jerry's weakness into a redeeming strength, and he can do the same for you. When you lean into the calling of the Holy Spirit, God will save you from yourself so you can do the same for others.

Follow the Call

Though God is totally capable of doing good work without our help, that is not his desire. He wants to work with us, refine us, and mold us into people who reflect his image—people who will be his hands and feet in the world. "For we are God's handiwork, created in Christ Jesus to do good works, which God prepared in advance for us to do" (Ephesians 2:10). Not only do we damage our own souls when we ignore spiritual intuitions, but we also damage the souls of those God planned for us to serve.

I used the same dry cleaner for twelve years. It didn't matter whether I visited in the morning or afternoon, on a weekday or a weekend, Ms. Kim was always there. She wasn't the owner; she was the lone employee. Occasionally, I would take Ms. Kim some of my baked goods. Though she always seemed grateful, I couldn't say for certain whether she ever ate anything. She was so very thin!

Because she did not speak English well, Ms. Kim was a woman of few words. However, her observation skills were unparalleled. Before a customer reached the counter with their ticket in hand, she would have their dry-cleaned clothes waiting for them on the rack. Despite the language barrier, I managed to learn that Ms. Kim was a widow with an estranged daughter living somewhere in New York City.

One morning when I stopped at the store, Ms. Kim failed to have my clothes waiting for me. She seemed confused and asked for my ticket. I paid for my order, wished her a good day, and left. But no sooner did I sit down in my car when my stomach turned. I recognized it as a spiritual nudge—one I did not readily welcome. I was busy. I had other errands to run.

Still, I took a moment to pray, which only served to increase the force of the nudge. According to pastor and author Mark Batterson, "A nudge is a means of encouraging and guiding behavior without mandating or instructing it. And it's evidence that small changes in input can make dramatic differences in outcome."[10]

I headed back inside.

"Ms. Kim," I said, "I don't think you're well. May I take you to the clinic down the road?" She wasn't sure what I was saying at first, but after several hand gestures and strange facial expressions, she agreed to go with me.

Within minutes of our arrival, the attending physician called an ambulance. Ms. Kim was admitted to the hospital, where she was diagnosed with Interstitial Lung Disease, an irreversible and progressive condition that causes stiffness in the lungs that makes it difficult to breathe. Thanks to technology, Ms. Kim was able to get her questions answered through a translator. Everything was being handled beautifully until I heard myself saying that I would help navigate Ms. Kim's medical appointments until we could find her daughter. I must have thought this would be easy. It was not.

It had been years since Ms. Kim had spoken to her only child, and she no longer knew where Jenny lived or how to get in touch with her. Consequently, I ended up making all of Ms. Kim's doctor appointments and driving her to every one of them. I could have abandoned her at any time, but I had made a commitment to Ms. Kim and to God.

Over the course of a year, I came to care deeply about Ms. Kim. We often shared lunch after an appointment, and it was during this time that I learned about her childhood in Korea, her arranged and abusive marriage, her escape to the United States, and her employment at the dry cleaners. My heart ached over the pain she carried from the past and the loneliness she felt in the present.

As her health deteriorated, the urgency to find Ms. Kim's daughter increased. I couldn't imagine what drove these two women apart. But whatever the wedge, I felt that Jenny had a right to know of her mother's condition. I could not rest until I found her.

"Am I going to die?" Ms. Kim would ask.

My answer was always the same. "Not yet! Not until we find your daughter!"

About a year after Ms. Kim's initial diagnosis, she was admitted to the hospital with a dire prognosis. Now when she asked, "Am I going to die?" I answered, "Probably."

Ms. Kim did not want to die in the hospital. She wanted to go home, but no doctor would release her. The oxygen from the hospital ventilator was the only thing keeping her alive. I visited as often as possible, but deep down, I knew I wasn't enough. Though I had grown to love and care for this woman, I was not family. I was not Jenny.

One day, I arrived at the hospital to learn that Ms. Kim had named me as her medical power of attorney. All I had to do was sign the papers. It was true that no one knew Ms. Kim's condition as well as I did, but I did not feel I had the right to make her end-of-life decisions. "She wants you to," the doctor replied. "She didn't name anyone else."

I wasn't convinced. I entered Ms. Kim's room to discuss the request. She met me with a huge smile. Then, turning to the doctor, Ms. Kim said in broken English, "She my angel!"

There was nothing to discuss. I signed the papers.

Failure to Respond

Why God chose me to care for Ms. Kim is both a mystery and an honor. I've often wondered whether other clients found her in distress at the drycleaners before I arrived or if I was the only one God had called to action. I'll never know the answer, but I like to think that this was a task God had prepared in advance for me alone. "And we know that in all things God works for the good of those who love him, who have been called according to his purpose" (Romans 8:28).

In a strange series of events with a hospital interpreter and a Korean social media app, I finally obtained a possible phone number for Ms. Kim's daughter. I nestled into the corner of a quiet hallway and tapped the digits into my cell phone. After several rings, I got an answering machine.

"You don't know me," I said, "but I'm a friend of your mother's."

I didn't go into detail because I wasn't sure I had the right person, but I left my number, hoping for a return call. Then I went back to Ms. Kim's hospital room to collect her personal items before she was transported to a hospice center thirty miles away. There was nothing more the doctors could do for her except make her comfortable for death. As I headed to my car, my cell phone rang.

God does indeed work in mysterious ways. Had I not signed the medical POA papers, I would not have had access to Ms. Kim's cell phone, the hospital's social worker, and the Korean interpreter, which all played a part in the reunion that was about to take place. Ms. Kim's daughter was not the disgruntled child her mother made her out to be. She was emotional, concerned, and embarrassed. Though I will never know what drove these two apart, imminent death drove them back together.

Several hours later, I picked Jenny up from the train station and drove her to the hospice facility. Her mother had been in and out of consciousness for several days, but when we walked into the room, Ms. Kim was wide awake. Her weak but precious smile for me faded into amazement as her eyes shifted to her daughter. The walls of misunderstanding fell as Jenny rushed forward into the open arms of her dying mother.

Witnessing this heartfelt reunion was a sacred moment that I will always treasure. Though I couldn't understand the rapid-fire Korean dialogue that passed between them, it was full of sorrow and love. Through tears, I quietly exited the room, knowing full well that I had accomplished what God had called me to do.

The next morning, I found Jenny curled up on the bed beside her mother, who had slipped into a coma. No longer able to hold her daughter, her daughter now held her.

I can't presume to know the outcome of a nudge ignored, but I will speculate. Had Jerry not entered that church when he heard the music, he would have checked himself into the detox center the next morning—unless he overdosed or was arrested first. Had

I not responded to the nudge at the dry cleaners, Ms. Kim would have passed away without her daughter's knowledge.

It's not enough to remain open to the gut feelings, spiritual inspirations, and intuitive signals God sends our way; we must act on them. What God calls us to do may not be what we expected, but the ride will be thrilling if we place our rational minds in the backseat and let the Holy Spirit drive.

GO DEEPER

Our minds are forever planning for the future or assessing the past. Rarely do we observe and enjoy the moment at hand. Yet Jesus encouraged us to live in the present moment when he said, "Can any one of you by worrying add a single hour to your life?" (Matthew 6:27).

To live in the present moment provides the space necessary to recognize God's presence. So, slow down and push distractions aside. Settle into a comfortable sitting position, close your eyes, and breathe deeply. Now take inventory of your surroundings with awareness and curiosity.

What do you hear? What sounds are new to you? Is there a sound you can't place? What might it be?

How does the world feel around your body? Is the chair comfortable beneath you? Does any part of your clothing irritate you? How is the temperature of the room?

Can you pick up on any scents? Where is this smell coming from? What does it remind you of?

How does your body feel internally? Where are you holding any stress? Does any part of you ache? Does your heart feel light or heavy? Is your stomach calm or churning? Is your jaw relaxed or clenched?

Ask God to enter the area that is giving you difficulty, reveal his truth, and guide you through it. "I plead with you to give your bodies to God because of all he has done for you. Let them be a living and holy sacrifice—the kind he will find acceptable. This is truly the way to worship him. Don't copy the behavior and customs of this world, but let God transform you into a new person by changing the way you think. Then you will learn to know God's will for you, which is good and pleasing and perfect" (Romans 12:1-2 NLT).

Sit in this moment with God for as long as you are able. Before opening your eyes, thank the Holy Spirit for whatever thoughts and feelings were revealed to you. As you go through the rest of your day, focus on living in the moment by paying attention to your senses.

Chapter 5

Doors: One Closes and Another Opens

When they came to the border of Mysia, they tried to enter Bithynia, but the Spirit of Jesus would not allow them to.

—Acts 16:7

Mary Anne had a three-step plan. She was going to leave Cincinnati, obtain an art degree in New York City, and land a prestigious job on the east coast designing textiles. There was no reason to believe she wouldn't achieve her goals. Mary Anne was smart, artistic, and resourceful.

When she graduated from high school, Mary Anne had her pick of colleges, but only one offered a revolutionary co-op program for design: the University of Cincinnati. Strike one.

During her sophomore year, she took a trip to NYC to meet with fashion professionals. The Vice President at Burlington Industries told Mary Anne he loved her work, but he wouldn't hire her based on where the market was headed. "Look, I've got artists that have no understanding about how business works. They're just creative," he told her. "Switch to marketing." Mary Anne returned to school and changed her major. Strike two.

When she graduated, Mary Anne accepted an invitation from a friend to interview with Procter & Gamble. She took the required test and achieved a perfect score. Two hours after her interview, the director called and offered her a sales position. Mary Anne turned him down. He refused to take "no" for an answer. A month later, Mary Anne was working for P&G in Michigan, nowhere near the east coast. Strike three.

We can make plans, set goals, and identify the markers of success, but there is no guarantee we will achieve any of them. "Many are the plans in a person's heart, but it is the Lord's purpose that prevails" (Proverbs 19:21).

The Holy Spirit as GPS

Over a span of about fifteen years, the apostle Paul traveled some 10,000 miles from Jerusalem to Athens and everywhere in between. With no public transit, no street signs or tour guides, and certainly no GPS, Paul relied fully on the Holy Spirit to map his route. The Bible tells us that while Barnabas and Paul were worshiping the Lord and fasting with other prophets from the church in Antioch, "the Holy Spirit said, 'Set apart for me Barnabas and Saul for the work to which I have called them.' So after they had fasted and prayed, they placed their hands on them and sent them off. The two of them, sent on their way by the Holy Spirit, went down to Seleucia and sailed from there to Cyprus" (Acts 13:2-4). Talk about the ultimate travel agent!

The journey was not always easy—in fact, it was downright difficult at times due to beatings, hunger, bandits, and shipwrecks. But Paul obediently walked through the doors that opened, trusting that God would make a way where there appeared to be no way.

Like Paul, Mary Anne followed a route she did not map out. The doors she approached closed while others opened. Positions were offered that she did not seek. But even as a teen, Mary Anne was prayerful and recognized that God was present in her journey.

As her professional status grew, Mary Anne went on to covertly, then intentionally, change the culture of the business environment at her company by making it safer and easier for women and diverse persons to ascend the corporate ladder. Her reputation spread, and later, other companies hired Mary Anne to coach them on strategic planning and organizational effectiveness. She eventually left P&G to open her own corporate consulting and executive coaching business, which gave her the platform necessary to make an even greater impact.

Using Our Gifts for God's Purposes

Why Paul? Why Mary Anne? Because God designed them for this.

Paul was a well-educated Roman citizen. He could think and write in Greek, Hebrew, and Aramaic, and he was well-versed in Scripture, which he used strategically to support his arguments for Christ as God's son. Trained as a tentmaker, Paul was able to support himself on his missionary journeys. He had all the necessary characteristics to carry out God's plan to spread the good news about Jesus to the Gentiles.

Mary Anne was a citizen of Cincinnati and familiar with Procter & Gamble, one of the main employers of the city. Smart, hardworking, unshakeable, and artistic—Mary Anne possessed a dangerous combination for a female executive in a man's world! She also got bored easily. The only time she escaped boredom was when she was creating. This made her the perfect candidate to bring lasting change to the corporate world through global innovations, shifts in business culture mindsets, and expanded opportunities for women and minorities.

Looking back, Mary Anne says not only does she see that the open doors were part of God's plan, but she also recognizes that the closed doors were a blessing in disguise. The design world she had hoped to enter at the time of her graduation was a hotbed of sexual promiscuity and illegal drugs. As a young Christian, it was a culture Mary Anne would not have been comfortable navigating. "God protected me," she says.

God may have protected her, but Mary Anne played her part by being obedient. As she puts it, "God opened the doors, and I walked through them, sat my butt down, and did what he said to do."

God designed each person with certain skills, traits, and propensities that prepare them for the good works he always planned for them to accomplish. We may learn additional skills and talents along the way, but unless they were part of God's design, they might not play into his grand objective. There is a saying that goes like this: God doesn't call the equipped; he equips the called. It may be more accurate to say that God doesn't call the self-equipped; he calls those he equipped.

While each of us was born with a purpose, life often has a way of turning our focus toward worldly agendas rather than spiritual goals. We buy into the media's lie that good enough is not really good enough. This leads us to buy the latest gadgets, lose weight, dye our hair, and spend money we don't have on things we don't need. We idolize the rich and famous and pursue careers that will make us the most money thinking that will make us happy. We dress ourselves in a false identity that doesn't quite fit and wonder why we feel unsatisfied. God does not want us to suffer as people the world says we should become; he wants us to thrive as the individuals he created each of us to be.

When we stray from God's plan, he will move mountains to get us back on track. The prophet Jeremiah wrote, "I went down to the potter's house, and I saw him working at the wheel. But the pot he was shaping from the clay was marred in his hands; so the potter formed it into another pot, shaping it as seemed best to him. Then the word of the Lord came to me. He said, 'Can I not do with you, Israel, as this potter does?' declares the Lord. 'Like clay in the hand of the potter, so are you in my hand, Israel'" (Jeremiah 18:3-5).

Not only was the nation of Israel subject to God's redesign when they strayed from their purpose, but we are too. Doors will close, and obstacles will appear. We may not like it, but it's for our own good and God's glory.

Doors That Open

I love having a car door opened for me. It makes me feel special. This is what God does for each of us when we follow the route he designed. Doors open. Sometimes it's one door, and sometimes it's multiple doors.

Lori was working part-time as a preschool teacher in a church when her marriage fell apart. Faced with a divorce she did not want and newfound financial hardship, Lori would have to seek more lucrative employment to keep a roof over her head. She wasn't, however, willing to compromise her values and beliefs just to make more money. She prayed for God's guidance.

A door opened when a friend offered Lori and her teenage daughter a room in her house for free until Lori could find the right full-time job. Accommodations were small, but they provided a safe, comfortable space where Lori and her daughter could grieve and heal.

Six months later, another door opened when Lori received funds from the sale of her marital house. She and her daughter could now move out of the free room and into a place of their own. Convinced she did not have enough money for a down payment on a house, Lori began to look at rental properties.

One day, while scanning through the options online, a home popped up that was listed for sale. "That's strange," Lori thought. "Why is a sale listing appearing on a rental page?" Lori clicked the ad and scanned the details. Not only was the house cute, but it was also affordable. Lori called a realtor friend to ask for a walkthrough.

The minute she walked through the front door, Lori knew she wanted to live in this house because it felt like home. Each step revealed another inviting room. If anything, the place was too large because it had an office that Lori didn't need. Lori made an offer.

Later that day, Lori learned that someone else had also put a bid on the house. If a bidding war started, she wouldn't be able to stay in the fight. Lori prayed, "Please, Lord, let the owners pick me, but only if it is your will." Though she knew the house was the right place for her daughter and her, Lori was also willing to let it go if God had other plans.

It didn't take long. Hours later, the realtor called to tell Lori that the owner had accepted her offer. Come to find out, the owner was a pastor. God had opened another door.

Soon after the move-in, Lori's job search took a turn when she interviewed for a full-time position at a Christian publishing company. One of the questions she was asked during the interview was, "Do you have a home office?" The very room Lori didn't think she needed was exactly what she did need.

"God is constantly surprising me with things," Lori says. "I think, 'I don't need that,' but he knows I do."

When we surrender to God's control, he will provide for us in ways we are unable to provide for ourselves. If it is God's will, the path forward will unfold easily. If it is not God's will, it will feel like pushing a rock up a hill. Bear in mind, however, that an easily unfolding path does not necessarily signify an uncomplicated journey. The spiritual battle for your soul is never-ending. If a storm arises, pause, pray, and wait. The correct path forward might not reveal itself for days, maybe years. But trust that when the time is right, God will provide an open door. When he does, walk through it without worry or fear, even if it's not the door you were expecting.

Unexpected Doors

Melissa was employed part-time as the Children's Ministry Director at the same Floridian church in which she had grown up. She loved both her job and the neighborhood that was so familiar to her. But when the pastor changed, Melissa was given additional duties that were outside of her job description. As a wife and mother of three young children, she could not sustain the demands of working full-time for part-time pay. She prayed daily for change, confident that God would hold true to his promise. "This is the confidence we have in approaching God: that if we ask anything according to his will, he hears us" (1 John 5:14).

At church one Sunday, Melissa was asked to put a stop to an ad that was running in the diocesan newsletter. It wasn't her job to oversee ads or deal with the diocese, but she respectfully did as she was asked. Scanning the newsletter in search of the ad in question, her eyes landed on a job opening: Director of Children's Ministry. Melissa says, "My heart leapt within me."

But then the location caught her eye: Virginia. That would never work with the lifestyle Melissa and her husband had built over the years. Her husband owned an antique business, and her extended family lived nearby. Melissa didn't want to leave her home. Even though the job sounded perfect, she laid the newsletter aside.

Day after day, Melissa sat with the Lord to pray that he would either relieve her of the additional duties at her current church or provide her with a Children's Ministry position at a different church. "Please, God," she pleaded, "open a door."

God's answer came through loud and clear. "I've already opened the door, Melissa. You need to walk through it."

Sometimes a door is covered with jewels, and we eagerly push it open to see what is on the other side. Other times, a door appears to be laden with splinters, and we pull back, unwillingly to risk getting a sliver. That was the kind of door Melissa was facing. She circled the ad in the newsletter and brought it to her husband. He read slowly, then raised his eyes to meet hers. "They've written your resume," he said. Reluctantly, Melissa applied for the job.

If God calls you to step out in faith, you need to be obedient. Many times, the apostle Paul was called to step out in faith. Even though he had an intimate and personal relationship with Christ, he wasn't always privy to what he was walking into. He told the Ephesian elders, "And now, compelled by the Spirit, I am going to Jerusalem, not knowing what will happen to me there. I only know that in every city the Holy Spirit warns me that prison and hardships are facing me" (Acts 20:22-23).

While Melissa waited to hear from the church she had applied to in Virginia, her husband's antique business in Florida began to tank. The inventory he had depended on from Europe mysteriously dried up. If Melissa was expecting a sign from God, this was it. In the months ahead, Melissa would fly to Virginia three times for interviews while her husband liquidated his company. When the Family Ministry Director position was finally offered to her, there was nothing left to hold Melissa back. She accepted the job.

The move turned out to be a blessing in disguise. Having lived in the same neighborhood since childhood and having worked in the same church in which she grew up, Melissa was unaware that she was in a spiritual rut. The church God had called her to in Virginia was rich in discipleship, where members were placed in home groups for fellowship and in Bible studies for spiritual growth. Kids participated in youth group, and service projects brought all ages together to care for the community and each other. In addition, northern Virginia offered excellent education options for the kids and exposed the whole family to the beauty of ethnic diversity. It was a glimpse of heaven on earth. The icing on the cake was when Melissa's husband was offered a job in Virginia weeks before he arrived. This was further confirmation that the move was orchestrated by a heavenly conductor.

God was growing and strengthening Melissa's faith for a purpose. Under her leadership, the children's ministry grew to become a model program for other churches in the area, and she went on to head the children's ministry program at a regional conference in her diocese. Melissa's leadership skills, love of children, can-do attitude, and strong faith were just what God needed to grow his kingdom in northern Virginia. It didn't happen overnight, but it rolled out in God's perfect time.

Doors that Close

It can be disheartening and downright frustrating to work hard for something and not attain the goal. Then we wonder why God allowed us to put in so much effort for little or no return. In times like this, you need to remember that God sees the big picture. If he brought you through one door only to close the next, some divine purpose was accomplished.

Jan and her husband, Karl, were nearing the end of a three-year military assignment in the Philippines. As the young couple prepared to return to the States, President Ferdinand Marcos' popularity was in steep decline. The Filipinos who showed up to pack Jan and Karl's belongings fought verbally with the hired help who had served the couple during their stay. Because Jan did not speak Tagalog, she had no idea what everyone was arguing about, but it made her feel uncomfortable.

In order to catch their early morning flight to Hong Kong, Jan and Karl would have to spend the night in Manila. Jan had always wanted to stay at the world-famous Manila Hotel with its marble floors and impressive chandeliers. Here was her chance.

The hotel was built at the request of William Howard Taft back when the U.S. was charged with organizing a civil government in the islands following the Spanish-American War of 1898. Over the years, a number of illustrious guests stayed in this five-star hotel, including General Douglas MacArthur, Ernest Hemingway, John Wayne, the Rockefeller brothers, the Beatles, and Michael Jackson. Jan looked forward to saying that she had stayed there, too!

But things did not work out as planned. For some unknown reason, Karl was unable to secure a room at the famed hotel. "How is it possible," Jan wondered, "that not one of the 600 rooms is available for one night?" The couple ended up spending their last night in the Philippines at the Plaza Hotel, which was closer to the airport.

The next morning, Jan and Karl boarded a plane to Hong Kong, where they would spend a couple of nights before catching a flight home to the U.S. The flight was uneventful and the taxi ride to the hotel was quick. While Karl checked in, Jan read the English captions on the TV screen in the lobby: *Revolution in the Philippines. Marcos overthrown.*

While Jan and Karl were enjoying their stay at the Plaza, demonstrators stormed the Manila Hotel in protest of Ferdinand Marcos' presidency. Marcos was not in the hotel at the time, but that didn't stop protestors from harassing guests and sending the city into chaos. Had Jan and Karl secured a room in that historic building, they would never have made it out of Manila in a timely fashion—perhaps not at all. God protected them from getting caught in a situation they did not even know existed. Such is the gift of a closed door.

Let God Navigate

Open doors align us with God's will, provide a direct path forward, and keep us safe. Therefore, walk through them. Closed doors protect us from unknown evils, pains, and disasters. Therefore, stop pushing if you encounter one. Though it is hard not to push when you desire what is on the other side, it is in your best interest to submit to God's will. God's timing is perfect, so it is possible that a closed door will open at a future time.

Consider Paul's response to the Jews in Ephesus when they asked him to remain with them a little longer. He declined. God made it clear to Paul that it was time for him to move on. "But as he left, he promised, 'I will come back if it is God's will.' Then he set sail from Ephesus" (Acts 18:21).

Paul did not stay when God wanted him to move. He obeyed. However, that locked door did not remain locked forever. On his third missionary journey, Paul returned to Ephesus, where he remained with the Ephesians for over two years.

Seek God's will. You certainly can ask friends for their help, but your best guide is God. He is waiting for you to ask for his direction, and he promises to respond. "Your own ears will hear him. Right behind you a voice will say, 'This is the way you should go,' whether to the right or to the left" (Isaiah 30:21 NLT).

God alone possesses the ultimate roadmap for your life, and you are in for an amazing journey if you allow him to navigate!

GO DEEPER

John Calvin, who is regarded as one of the most influential Protestant theologians, wrote, "Our wisdom, in so far as it ought to be deemed true and solid Wisdom, consists almost entirely of two parts: the knowledge of God and of ourselves."[11] There is no one more qualified to teach you about yourself than God. He knows you better than you do.

When Jesus saw Nathanael for the first time, he said, "Here truly is an Israelite in whom there is no deceit" (John 1:47). Jesus was saying that Nathanael was upright, honest, and genuine. Jesus saw into Nathanael's heart and found him to be a man who was exactly who God had created him to be.

It is easier to recognize both closed and open doors when we are living into our true selves. When we don masks that we hope will make us appear more important, smarter, richer, or stronger than we really are, our sight becomes skewed, and our paths become crooked.

Take an honest look at yourself. Do you act the same way at home as you do at work? Would a church member be shocked if they ran into you on a Saturday night? Is there anything you do in secret that you hope no one ever discovers? Do you hide behind fear, shame, or insecurity? Have you ever pretended to be more important, smarter, richer, or stronger than you really are?

I find it helpful to journal about my self-discoveries and lay them before the Lord in prayer. He, of course, already knows everything there is to know about me, but naming and placing my mask before God demonstrates that I am aware of my lies, too. Together, we can uncover the truth in my heart, which paves the way for wholeness and honesty. One thing living through the COVID-19 pandemic has taught me is that it is much easier to breathe when I'm not wearing a mask.

Getting to know yourself can be scary, but it is a surefire way to build intimacy with God.

Chapter 6

Surroundings: Signs and Coincidences

For by him all things were created:
things in heaven and on earth, visible and invisible,
whether thrones or powers or rulers or authorities;
all things were created by him and for him.

—Colossians 1:16

I was on my way to the daytime homeless shelter where I had volunteered to teach a weekly Bible study. This first visit was to acclimate me to the people and process by sitting in on another teacher's lesson.

The two-story building sat on a dead-end street lined with car repair shops. It wasn't exactly inviting, but it wasn't intimidating either. The front doors opened into a large room dominated by a long, stationary table where a number of people sat waiting for the lesson to begin. An employee named Dave introduced himself and then introduced me to some of the people. It was hard to tell the guests from the staff. I casually took a seat at the far end of the table where I could watch without participating.

The lesson that day was on Psalm 23, which is one of two Psalms I have memorized. My favorite line comes at the end of verse four. "Your rod and your staff, they comfort me." The rod symbolizes authority and would have been used by shepherds to fight off predators. The staff symbolizes support and would have been used to guide sheep along the right path. As the psalmist stated, it is comforting to know that God is both our guide and our protector.

About halfway through the lesson, my phone rang. All eyes turned toward me. (So much for remaining inconspicuous!) Noting it was my sister's number, I quickly hurried outside to answer the call.

"Mom had another stroke."

Our mother had been in a nursing home for over three years following a stroke that left her paralyzed on one side. She could no longer speak, but she recognized her family and always had a smile to share. My sister and father had been called into the nursing home earlier that morning when the staff recognized something was wrong.

"How is she doing?" I asked.

"Not good," my sister answered. "The priest was just here. He recited the twenty-third psalm over her."

Though my mom was three states away, I felt a spiritual connection through Scripture. Of the hundreds of passages in the Bible, my sister and I were hearing the same words at the same time. It was comforting to know we were on the same page.

I returned to the table just as the lesson was ending. Dave asked, "Does anyone have any prayer requests?"

"I do," I answered. (I was failing miserably at maintaining a low profile.) "I just received a call from my sister. My mom is dying."

"What is her name?" someone asked.

"Her name is Loretta."

Dave stared at me, a strange expression on his face. "Did you say 'Loretta'?" he asked with a tinge of disbelief.

That morning, as Dave drove into work, he had a strong feeling come over him to pray for a former girlfriend's mother. He hadn't seen this girl or her mother in years. In fact, he was now married to someone else and had recently become a father. "Why," he wondered, "is God asking me to pray for Loretta?" Though it didn't make sense at the time, Dave did as he felt called.

I had never met Dave before that morning. He knew nothing about my mother. Yet through the leading of the Holy Spirit, he had prayed for her by name. This was no coincidence. I knew that Mom's time on earth was nearing its end, and yet I felt strangely at peace because God had given me not one but two signs.

The Writing on the Wall

Our world is full of signs. They display the names of streets or the distance to the next town. They tell us to stop or yield. They warn of detours or road work. Signs of this sort did not exist when the Bible was being written. So, when Scripture speaks of signs, it is referring to a mark of divine power, such as a healing, a sudden change in weather, or the visible indication of an invisible presence.

People of the ancient world believed in a spiritual realm and attributed unexplainable occurrences to the gods. Over the centuries, as science evolved along with our ability to explain certain phenomena, humankind's belief in the supernatural waned. Though miracles and divine incidents still happen today, most of us Westerners do not even consider God as their source. Instead, we acknowledge them as coincidences.

Let's take a moment to look at the writing on the wall.

King Belshazzar held a great banquet for thousands of guests. At this banquet, he ordered his servants to serve wine in the goblets that his late father, Nebuchadnezzar, removed from the temple in Jerusalem. "As they drank the wine, they praised the gods of gold and silver, of bronze, iron, wood, and stone. Suddenly the fingers of a human hand appeared and wrote on the plaster of the wall near the lampstand in the royal palace. The king watched the hand as it wrote. His face turned pale, and he was so frightened that his legs became weak and his knees were knocking" (Daniel 5:4-6).

If this happened today, we would think a magician was involved, or we might consider attributing the action to a ghost. For Belshazzar, the only explanation was the supernatural. Having just praised the gods of various metals and minerals, the king probably considered one of them responsible for the writing. Whatever the source, he needed someone to decipher the inscription so he could respond to it. MENE, MENE, TEKEL, PARSIN.

Enchanters and astrologers were called in, but they could not explain the meaning of the strange words. King Belshazzar became more terrified because messages from the gods were not to be ignored. Was there anyone in the kingdom who could translate the writing on the wall?

Apparently, there was. The queen knew of a man named Daniel, an exile from Jerusalem who had escaped from the lion's den. Not only did he possess a keen mind and the ability to solve riddles, but he also had "the spirit of the holy gods in him" (Daniel 5:11).

Daniel was found and brought before the king. He displayed no hesitation in delivering the convicting interpretation of the words. "You have set yourself up against the Lord of heaven. You had the goblets from his temple brought to you, and you and your nobles, your wives and your concubines drank wine from them. You praised the gods of silver and gold, of bronze, iron, wood and stone, which cannot see or hear or understand. But you did not honor the God who holds in his hand your life and all your ways" (Daniel 5:23).

Daniel went on to tell King Belshazzar that his days were numbered and that Babylon was headed for destruction. The interpretation proved to be spot on. That very night, Darius the Mede invaded Babylon, killed Belshazzar, and took over the kingdom.

If Daniel had not been called to the palace to interpret the writing, King Belshazzar would still have been killed, but he and his entourage would not have known why. As God would have it, the king went to his death with the full knowledge of his sin, and every guest learned that the power of life and death belonged to God alone.

Diviners, Mystics, and Fortune Tellers

Every time I pass a place that advertises tarot cards or palm readings, I get the creeps. I don't doubt that some of them are legitimate since fortune tellers have been around since the beginning of time, but most do not speak for God.

Consider the female slave in the Book of Acts who made money for her owners by predicting the future. When the apostle Paul was released from prison, she followed him and his companions around, shouting to the crowd, "These men are servants of the Most High God who are telling you the way to be saved" (Acts 16:17). She wasn't wrong, but her motives were. Each prediction was subject to payment. She was not sharing the good news of Christ to bring him glory but to bring her owners fame and riches. It's no wonder that Paul finally got fed up with her shouting and turned to confront not the woman but the spirit within. "'In the name of Jesus Christ, I command you to come out of her!' At that moment the spirit left her" (Acts 16:18).

We need to be careful about whom we listen to and, even more importantly, whom we follow. Signs from God are best interpreted with the help of God-fearing people. A mystic *might* be able to decipher a sign from God, but it is unlikely that her words will align with God's will.

Years ago, I had a conversation with a telemarketer who was trying to sell me a publishing package. The company Karen represented was billed as a Christian company, but I didn't get the feeling that she was Christian. I listened respectfully, asked some questions, and then politely declined the offer. Instead of hanging up, however, Karen asked if we could keep talking. I said a quick prayer and felt God telling me to keep the conversation going.

That one conversation led to another and to another. Over the course of four phone calls (all initiated by Karen), I came to find out that she was Jewish and frequented a tarot card reader. When I asked her why, she told me that the information this woman provided was always accurate. I didn't doubt it.

"God is always speaking," I told her, "but I think you could find spiritual clarity without paying for it." She was intrigued, so I asked, "Do you see any patterns in your life that show up over and over again?"

"Yes!" She said, "I see the numbers 3-1-6 everywhere!"

"Did you ask your tarot card reader about this?"

She said she had, but the woman had no explanation for these numbers. Her advice was that Karen keep paying attention to when and where the numbers appeared and to keep coming back to her to see if a meaning would surface.

Some of you may see what I saw. John 3:16 says, "For God so loved the world that He gave his one and only Son, that whoever believes in him shall not perish but have eternal life." I shared this Scripture passage with Karen. I told her that she was beloved by God, and he wanted her to know it. She thought that was cool, but she was not interested in learning anything more about Jesus or Christianity. I would have liked to share more, but Karen was not ready to hear what I wanted to say, and the Holy Spirit was telling me not to push.

Karen and I no longer talk on the phone, but we follow each other on social media. I suspect she is still frequenting her tarot card reader, but I don't believe our conversations were in vain. Because there are no coincidences with God, I trust he placed me in Karen's life for one purpose: to plant a seed that someone else will water down the road.

Clarity, Confirmation, or Proof

Like Karen, not everyone in the Bible is pleased to hear from God. Most are either confused by what they've heard and ask for clarity, or they are uncertain that God is doing the talking and ask for confirmation.

Consider Mary's response when an angel of the Lord tells her that she is going to bear God's child. She asks for clarity. "But how can this happen? I am a virgin" (Luke 1:34 NLT). Though Mary was greatly troubled over getting pregnant without a husband, she listened as the angel explained how the Holy Spirit would come to her and the power of the Most High would overshadow her. Mary responds with, "I am a servant of the Lord; let this happen to me according to your word" (Luke 1:38 NET). Mary shows us that asking for clarity demonstrates a desire to respond to God's directive correctly.

Gideon, a ruling judge of Israel before the nation had a king, also asked for clarity, but he followed this up with a request for confirmation.

Surrounding tribes from Midian and Canaan oppressed the Israelites by killing their livestock and ruining their crops. The people cried out to God for help. That's when an angel of the Lord appeared to Gideon and told him, "Go with the strength you have and rescue Israel from the Midianites. I am sending you!" (Judges 6:14 NLT).

The first question Gideon asked was for clarity. How was he to accomplish this task since he was the youngest in his family and his clan was the weakest in Manasseh? After the angel provided the answer, Gideon followed up with a request for confirmation. "Look, I will place a wool fleece on the threshing floor. If there is dew only on the fleece and all the ground is dry, then I will know that you will save Israel by my hand, as you said" (Judges 6:37). Gideon was not testing the Lord's word; he was confirming that the word came from God.

There is one more thing to note in this story. Between the clarity question and the confirmation exchange, Gideon sacrificed a bull to God using the wood of the Asherah pole to build a fire. The Asherah pole was a type of monument to a Canaanite goddess. Before Gideon dared to ask God to confirm his identity, he acknowledged his commitment to God through sacrifice. Gideon shows us that asking for confirmation is appropriate when a person's heart is in the right place.

So, what types of questions are unacceptable? Just one: asking God for proof of his existence when proof has already been provided. This is what Jesus was often up against.

Jesus turned water into wine, healed the sick, brought people back to life, and fed thousands with one basket of bread and a couple of fish. His miracles were numerous and occurred over several years. Yet the Pharisees and Sadducees demanded that he show them a sign from heaven to prove his authority. That's why Jesus responded, "Only an evil, adulterous generation would demand a miraculous sign, but the only sign I will give them is the sign of the prophet Jonah" (Matthew 16:4).

The religious rulers had been eyewitnesses to signs of divinity, yet they couldn't believe what they saw. We are no better if we accuse God of not hearing our prayers when he doesn't respond the way we want him to. God is not to be tested. We can ask for clarity or confirmation, but not proof. "But when you ask, you must believe and not doubt, because the one who doubts is like a wave of the sea, blown and tossed by the wind. That person should not expect to receive anything from the Lord" (James 1:6-7).

What's Your Sign?

God often speaks in "sign" language that gives us a glimpse of divinity and invites us into a conversation with him. Each person's sign is unique. I'm not talking about your zodiac sign; I'm talking about the sign God placed in your heart where his spirit can speak to your spirit.

Are you a musician? Perhaps God will speak to you through music. Do you read the newspaper each morning? Perhaps God will speak to you through the headlines. Do you ride the train to work every day? Perhaps God will speak to you through the graffiti or advertisements you see. He will meet you where you are.

My friend Denise lost her oldest sister in an unusual and tragic incident when an ovarian cyst ruptured. Her sudden death was a shock for the family of five girls because there had been no visible warning signs that anything was wrong.

After the funeral, the remaining sisters decided to do what they always did when they got together, and that was shop. They loaded into the car with their parents in tow and headed toward the stores. But venturing out during a time of grief seemed ridiculous. How could they go shopping without Regina? She was the queen bee, the one who drove the car and coordinated these events. Who would take charge in her absence?

The car was deathly quiet when someone suggested that they just head home. Perhaps that would be best. Shopping wasn't going to work without Regina.

The car stopped at a red light. Denise stared out the side window from the back seat. Her eyes drifted to the license plate on the car in the next lane. It said, "Queen Bee." Denise screamed! "Look, everyone!"

Gasps of surprise and cries of wonder filled the car. For just a moment, the pain slipped away as memories of Regina's queen bee prowess rippled through the vehicle. It was the sign everyone needed.

Since that encounter, God has continued to speak to Denise through license plates. She is a professional organizer and life coach, so a lot of her time is spent in the car driving from one client to another. As she drives, she talks with God. She asks him questions or just shares stories with him. It's quite common for a clarifying word or phrase to suddenly appear on a license plate in front of her, like CHOSN2B, 1GODSVS, and F8HFUL1. There is nothing to decipher; the answer is always clear. License plates are Denise's sign. She believes God uses them to tell her that he is listening and present in the conversation with her.

There Are No Coincidences

Recognizing a sign as confirmation of God's presence is a game changer. Once you catch on to how God is speaking to you, you will begin to seek him on a regular basis and find him more often. In addition, your conversations with God will flow more easily, and your spiritual eyes will notice God in more areas of your life.

In her book *Jesus Calling*, Sarah Young writes, "When you depend on me continually, your whole perspective changes. You see miracles happening all around, while others see only natural occurrences and 'coincidences.'"[12] When you learn how to read God's signs and accept them as invitations to communicate with him or act on his behalf, the outcomes are nothing short of miraculous.

Megan is a psychologist who took a mission trip to Bulgaria to learn more about human trafficking. In a Roma village, Megan and her guide, Dimitri, walked the unpaved roads talking to women about the despicable trade that was evident to everyone in the community.

One woman invited Megan into her home to talk. Sabina was fluent in English and shared stories she knew about women who worked for pimps and girls who had disappeared forever. "The village was small," Megan said, "and everybody knew everybody's business."

At the end of their conversation, Megan invited Sabina to attend the church service being held later that night, where she was a guest speaker. Sabina wasn't sure she could attend, but she asked Megan to pray for her. The young mother not only had a three-year-old daughter and a newborn son to care for, but she was also suffering from a bladder injury she incurred during her son's delivery.

That evening, Megan was surprised to see Sabina turn up for the service, and afterward, the two women went outside to talk. As they stood on the sidewalk sharing their concerns for the women in the village, Sabina's husband rounded the corner carrying the children. The little girl, unable to sleep, wanted her mother to come home.

Megan's eyes widened as they landed on the nightgown Sabina's daughter was wearing. It was the very same one that Megan's daughter wore and considered her favorite. This was not a common nightgown. Megan had acquired it at a yard sale years earlier when it was already off the market. Covered with butterflies, it was old but super soft, cheap but irreplaceable. At that moment, Megan felt connected to Sabina. This was the first time Megan had been away from her two girls since their birth, and she was missing them terribly. "God got my attention with that nightgown," Megan said. "So, I paid attention."

Megan went on to several other villages before she returned home to Virginia, and though she did not see Sabina again, she often popped into Megan's mind. When Megan spoke with Dimitri by phone several weeks later, she asked him, "Do you know how Sabina is doing?"

Dimitri didn't have an answer. He hadn't been back to that village since Megan's visit, but he promised he would keep his ears open for any information about the young mother.

The very next day, Dimitri paid a visit to the local hospital. When he missed his turn into the parking lot, he looped around and drove past the front door of the building. At that very moment, Sabina was walking out for a breath of fresh air. Within hours, Megan and Sabina were chatting on FaceTime.

Sabina had been admitted to the hospital with a bladder infection. Doctors told her that she needed neobladder reconstruction, which she could not afford. The prognosis was not good, and she was in much pain. To make matters worse, Sabina's husband was mad at God and at her.

Megan got to work. She sent emails to her friends and fellow church members asking for prayer and donations. Within ten days, Megan had raised enough money to pay for Sabina's surgery, which was performed immediately. When the surgeons opened her up, not only did they find urine leaking into her body, but they also found surgical equipment left behind from her previous operation. Had Megan not intervened, Sabina may not have survived the year, which would have left her two children motherless.

Megan's faithfulness in viewing the nightgown as a sign from God led to both physical and spiritual healing. Sabina felt her encounter with Megan had been divinely appointed, and she recommitted herself to God. In addition, Sabina's husband, who had never been a churchgoer, was now interested in learning more about the local church.

As Megan puts it, "When you have a desire to know God and open yourself up to being used by him, you eventually stop being surprised by coincidences. But I'm still tickled."

It was no coincidence that Jesus's death and resurrection mirrored the sign of Jonah, who spent three days in the belly of the whale before being returned to life. If God was willing to give his accusers this clear sign of his divinity (see Matthew 16:1-4), how much more will he give to those of us who believe?

GO DEEPER

Mark Batterson writes in his book, *Whisper*, "Ignoring signs is ignoring the God who speaks through them, and we do so to our own detriment."[13] God wants us to participate in his desire to bring hope, healing, and joy to a broken world. But we can't work on his behalf if we don't recognize his presence.

Start by having a conversation with God. Don't pray to him; talk with him. Approach God as you would a friend. Tell him what you're thinking and how you've planned your day. Ask him if your plans are compatible with his or if there is something that needs to change. Share a story or a concern you have. Take time to listen for his response. If it helps, sit at a table, and imagine Jesus sitting across from you. Ask him to give you a sign that he is with you. Then keep your eyes and ears open for an answer that might come in any shape or form.

In addition to nurturing your one-on-one relationship with Jesus, connect with others in a Christian community. This might mean joining a Bible study or volunteering at a church. Don't rule out starting your own small group that could focus on studying Scripture, reading Christian living books, practicing Christian disciplines, or supporting a specific cause. Jesus handpicked his disciples, so feel free to handpick the individuals you want to grow with spiritually.

The devil would like nothing more than to get you alone, separated from Christian community. Don't give him a foothold. Jesus said, "For where two or three gather in my name, there am I with them" (Matthew 18:20). Meet regularly with other believers. Share stories of how God is showing up in your lives. Identify the signs he uses to communicate with each of you. Pray for each other. "And let us consider how we may spur one another on toward love and good deeds, not giving up meeting together, as some are in the habit of doing, but encouraging one another—and all the more as you see the Day approaching" (Hebrews 10:25).

Chapter 7

The Voice: Hearing the Audible Words of God

The voice of the Lord is over the waters;
the God of glory thunders, the Lord thunders over the mighty waters.
The voice of the Lord is powerful; the voice of the Lord is majestic.

—Psalm 29:3-4

The visit to the Western Wall was the pinnacle of my trip to Jerusalem, not because of its historical significance but because of what I experienced there.

Built by Herod the Great to surround the Temple Mount, the Western Wall is considered by Jewish people today to be the holiest place on earth because of its proximity to the inner sanctuary of the Jewish Temple. Better known as the Holy of Holies, this is where God was thought to dwell on the earth.

Our Jewish guide informed us of the various methods visitors use to pray at the wall. Some write prayers on little pieces of paper that they wedge into the seams of the limestone. Others stand with their foreheads against the wall and pray. Some bring their own chair on which to sit for hours while touching the stone with one hand. We were warned to pay attention to the Jews who were leaving the area because they tended to exit backward, bowing as they departed, as if they were leaving the presence of a king.

Honoring God was my top priority, but I wasn't sure which approach would achieve this goal. I, therefore, decided the best thing to do was to copy my husband.

I nagged Greg all morning. "What are you going to do?" I asked. I wanted to know if he planned to look at the wall, touch it, or stick a prayer in it. Unfortunately, he hadn't decided, which left me unsettled on the day of our visit. Before boarding the tour bus, I wrote a prayer on a small piece of hotel paper and stuck it in my pocket so I would be prepared for every scenario.

As I boarded the tour bus for the short ride to the Western Wall, I started to pray. "Open my eyes so I can see visions of truth you have for me." This became my mantra.

When we arrived, our tour guide reminded us of the rules: Be respectful. Cover your shoulders. Keep your eyes open, and move out of the way of individuals exiting backward. Then he said, "Men line up over here; women over there."

What? I was being separated from my husband? Why hadn't I been informed of this earlier?

Gender segregation was established at the Western Wall in 1967 following the Six-Day War that expanded Israel's borders. Though most of the visitors were women, a much larger section of the wall was accessible to men only. I joined the women's line on the other side of a fabric partition that not only separated us from the men but also blocked our view of them.

"Open my eyes so I can see visions of truth you have for me."

I couldn't help but wonder if any of the apostles had passed this way. Perhaps John or Peter had brought an offering into this holy space where I now stood. Or maybe this was where Jesus had overturned the vendor stalls. I truly felt like I was walking on holy ground, but I did not believe that the wall itself held any special powers.

"Open my eyes so I can see visions of truth you have for me."

Some women walked quickly to the wall, stuck their prayers in it, and left as fast as they had arrived. Others, like me, walked forward slowly and respectfully. There were women who kissed the wall before departing and others who never touched it at all. I noticed several Jewish women sitting in chairs with their fingers spread wide against the stone, nodding their heads, and reciting prayers in a language I did not understand. Some wept. "Ah," I thought, "this is why it's called the Wailing Wall." I stepped aside for a woman walking backward, bowing as she withdrew.

"Open my eyes so I can see visions of truth you have for me."

Eight feet from the wall, panic gripped me. What was I supposed to do? How could I best honor God? "Open my eyes so I can see visions of truth you have for me."

I had a decision to make. I ran my fingers over the prayer in my pocket. Would God be offended if I stuck this little piece of paper in a limestone crack?

"Open my eyes so I can see visions of truth you have for me."

Should I at least touch the stone out of respect for the Jews?

"Open my eyes so I can see visions of truth you have for me. Open my eyes so I can see visions of truth you have for me."

And then I heard Him.

For just a moment, all other sounds vanished. It was as if I had entered a vacuum. In the total silence, the voice was clear and precise. Masculine but gentle. "I am not here. I am among the living."

My head snapped to the right and then to the left. I was standing among women. Not a single man was in sight. Standing in Jerusalem, just a few feet from the Wailing Wall, I half expected to see Jesus standing beside me. I stopped where I was and said a short prayer of gratitude. Then I turned my back on the wall and walked out.

This was not the first time I had heard God's voice—but it was the first time I recognized it.

Mistaken Identity

It's interesting to watch the reaction of a screaming child who has lost sight of his mother. Panic sets in as fearful eyes search for his safety net. When Mom comes into view, or he hears her voice, the screaming dies down and the whimpering begins, which indicates both relief and rebuke.

I recently became acquainted with my great-nephew, who was born to my niece during the COVID-19 pandemic. Less than two years old when we finally met, Michael practically choked his mother as he clung to her neck in fear that I might try to hold him. I kept a reasonable distance, which gave Michael time to calm down and sneak a peek at me. His skeptical eyes and furrowed brow informed me that we were not going to be immediate friends, even though I looked like an older version of his mother.

Several days later, while playing monster with his dad, Michael came running into the kitchen, screaming and laughing. He grabbed onto my legs, and I immediately scooped him up to protect him from the big bad monster. Keeping his eyes on his father, he failed to notice who it was that picked him up. But when I said, "Don't worry, Michael, I'll protect you," he let out a scream to wake the dead. My voice was not the one he expected. When he heard it, Michael knew he had run to the wrong person.

The voice of a stranger may evoke fear, while the voice of a loved one evokes comfort. But sometimes, we misidentify the voice.

> One night Eli, whose eyes were becoming so weak that he could barely see, was lying down in his usual place. The lamp of God had not yet gone out, and Samuel was lying down in the house of the Lord, where the ark of God was. Then the Lord called Samuel.
>
> Samuel answered, "Here I am." And he ran to Eli and said, "Here I am; you called me."
>
> But Eli said, "I did not call; go back and lie down." So he went and lay down.
>
> Again the Lord called, "Samuel!" And Samuel got up and went to Eli and said, "Here I am; you called me."

> "My son," Eli said, "I did not call; go back and lie down."
>
> Now Samuel did not yet know the Lord: The word of the Lord had not yet been revealed to him.
>
> A third time the Lord called, "Samuel!" And Samuel got up and went to Eli and said, "Here I am; you called me." (1 Samuel 3:2-8)

Samuel—raised in God's service under the watchful eye of the temple priest of Shiloh—misidentified the owner of the voice three times. Luckily, Samuel had a mentor who was able to point him in the right direction.

> Then Eli realized that the Lord was calling the boy. So Eli told Samuel, "Go and lie down, and if he calls you, say, 'Speak, Lord, for your servant is listening.'" So Samuel went and lay down in his place.
>
> The Lord came and stood there, calling as at the other times, "Samuel! Samuel!"
>
> Then Samuel said, "Speak, for your servant is listening." (1 Samuel 3:9-10)

The Bible tells us that the voice of God was rare in those days. Some might say it is rare in these days, too. But what if we're wrong? What if God is constantly talking and, like Samuel, we don't recognize the voice? It would be wonderful if we all had a mentor like Eli who could provide us with spiritual wisdom, but even Eli had to take the first step of getting to know God personally. This is what we need to do as well.

Until we establish a personal relationship with God, we will not be able to discern whether the voice we hear above the crowd is one we should run away from or run to.

Recognizing God's Verbal Characteristics

Samuel's eventual response to God's call was, "Speak, for your servant is listening." These are not words that reflect fear, doubt, or distrust. They are words that reflect commitment, respect, and obedience. Samuel may not have recognized God's voice at first, but he knew God's character. Therefore, when God shared an incriminating story with Samuel about Eli and his family (see 1 Samuel 3:11-14), Samuel believed and trusted not only the words he heard but the God who said them.

There are two distinct traits associated with the words God speaks. One, he cannot lie and, therefore, speaks only the truth. Two, God never contradicts himself. Jesus exemplified these character traits with every word he spoke. It didn't matter whether he was talking to his disciples or a Pharisee, a blind man or a possessed woman, a thief or a Roman official. Jesus' words resounded with truth, knowledge of the Father, and love. Because his character was flawless and consistent, he could be trusted then, and his words can still be trusted today.

Sadly, many people have gotten hung up on the details of the words spoken rather than the intention behind them. The Bible tells us that "the Pharisees went out and laid plans to trap him in his words" (Matthew 22:15). Instead of listening to Jesus with their hearts, they listened with their ears so they could discredit him. Had they focused more on his character, they would have recognized Jesus as the Son of God by the words he spoke. They claimed to know the truth about Jesus, but they were wrong. And Jesus called them out.

> "Very truly I tell you Pharisees, anyone who does not enter the sheep pen by the gate, but climbs in by some other way, is a thief and a robber. The one who enters by the gate is the shepherd of the sheep. The gatekeeper opens the gate for him, and the sheep listen to his voice. He calls his own

> sheep by name and leads them out. When he has brought out all his own, he goes on ahead of them, and his sheep follow him because they know his voice. But they will never follow a stranger; in fact, they will run away from him because they do not recognize a stranger's voice." Jesus used this figure of speech, but the Pharisees did not understand what he was telling them. (John 10:1-5)

In their defense, the Pharisees had limited knowledge of the one true God. Years of study had taught them to focus on the interpretation of the words in Scripture, not on nurturing a personal relationship with their creator. In essence, God was a stranger to them. They did not know God's character and were, therefore, unable to recognize his voice.

Meanwhile, twelve men were getting to know Jesus intimately as they spent quality time with him, day in and day out. They ate meals together, sat in the first row for all his lessons, and were eyewitnesses to his healings and miracles. It took time, but one day Peter was able to say with confidence, "You are the Messiah, the Son of the living God" (Matthew 16:16).

If you are adamant about recognizing Jesus' voice, ask God to transform your head knowledge into heart knowledge. While you wait, work on your personal relationship with God so that you will be able to recognize his voice if he decides to speak audibly to you.

The Audible Call of God

There is no guarantee that you will hear God's audible voice. There is no magic formula or secret incantation to make him talk. Even the most devout Christians are not able to summon God to speak. During a particularly dark period in Mother Teresa's ministry, she confessed to her spiritual confidant, Reverend Michael Van Der Peet, "Jesus has a very special love for you. [But] as for me—the silence and the emptiness are so great—that I look and do not see, –Listen and do not hear."[14]

My husband is another example of a committed Christian who has never heard the audible voice of God. However, it is not a desire of his heart to hear it. He is quite content with asking me to hear from God on his behalf whenever discernment is required. Not because I'm opinionated (which I am) or because I'm wiser (because that's questionable), but because I'm more adept at perceiving it in whatever form God chooses to use. However, having heard God's audible voice in the past, I know it's possible for me to hear it again in the future, and I believe I will. I can't force it, but I can ask for it.

God's Voice is Consistent

Back in 2001, Joan and her husband purchased a failing business from a wealthy entrepreneur. They threw their hearts and expertise into the venture, and three years later, they were able to sell the business to a large company at a great profit. When the original owner heard about the sale, he became insanely jealous and sued for compensation. Joan, who handled all the business records, had to provide documentation of the terms of the sale to prove their right to all the proceeds. The paperwork requested was excessive, and Joan felt both personally and spiritually attacked.

One day as she was heading into the basement to gather more files for the attorneys, she was overwhelmed by a loud voice. As Joan describes it, "It felt like it was coming from outside of me and inside of me." The voice was so loud she threw her hands over her ears, but the lyrics from the second verse of "How Firm a Foundation" could not be silenced.

> Fear not, I am with thee, O be not dismayed
> For I am thy God, and will still give thee aid;
> I'll strengthen thee, help thee, and cause thee to stand,
> Upheld by My righteous, omnipotent hand.[15]

As a longtime member of her church choir, Joan immediately recognized the hymn and the significance of the words, which came from the book of Isaiah, concerning Judah's captivity by the Babylonian Empire. "So do not fear, for I am with you; do not be dismayed, for I am your God. I will strengthen you and help you; I will uphold you with my righteous right hand" (Isaiah 41:10). Though Judah would be sacked, and its people exiled, God would redeem and restore them in due time.

God did the same for Joan. The lawsuit lingered for several more months, yet Joan was able to endure having been strengthened and supported through the words of Isaiah. She says, "God arrived when I needed him most and gave me peace."

It should come as no surprise that God used the lyrics from a beloved hymn to point Joan to Scripture. "All Scripture is inspired by God and is useful to teach us what is true and to make us realize what is wrong in our lives. It corrects us when we are wrong and teaches us to do what is right. God uses it to prepare and equip his people to do every good work" (2 Timothy 3:16-17 NLT).

God also spoke words that aligned with Scripture when he spoke to me at the Wailing Wall. His audible words did not contradict his character. "He is not the God of the dead, but of the living, for to him all are alive" (Luke 20:38).

God can certainly speak any words he chooses, but when he quotes Scripture, we are assured that the source is divine. And it doesn't matter whether God uses words from the Old Testament or the New Testament because all Scripture points to the Messiah. Jesus said, "Do not think that I have come to abolish the Law or the Prophets; I have not come to abolish them but to fulfill them. For truly I tell you, until heaven and earth disappear, not the smallest letter, not the least stroke of a pen, will by any means disappear from the Law until everything is accomplished" (Matthew 5:17-18).

The living Word of God is alive, active, and powerful. Whether you hear it audibly or not is up to God. Whether you recognize God as the source of that voice is up to you.

GO DEEPER

No matter how well you know Scripture, you can always delve deeper. Read the Bible for the sole purpose of getting to know Jesus better. Approach this task with excitement and awe, as if you were learning all about a brother you never knew you had.

First, enroll in a Bible study class led by someone who knows Scripture well. This direct approach holds participants accountable to daily reading while they gain insight into God's character, his promises, and how Christians are to act in the world. A good "study" or "life application" Bible will help you understand and implement what you are reading.

Second, study the Bible on your own. Compare the stories in the four gospels. Set a goal to read the Bible in a year, cover to cover or chronologically. See what scholars have to say about Jesus's ministry. Explore interpretations of various readings. Research the meaning of difficult sentences. Examine the prophecies and when they were fulfilled.

Third, use Scripture. Read it out loud. Memorize a new phrase each week and recite it often as your mantra. Retell a Scripture story to someone else using your own words. Journal your thoughts on passages that stirred your heart. Add a favorite line of Scripture to your email signature.

Above all, never stop learning. Theodore Roosevelt once said, "A thorough knowledge of the Bible is worth more than a college education." I couldn't agree more!

Get to know this God of mercy and love intimately so you are clear on what the Bible says and doesn't say, what it means and what it doesn't mean. You may not hear God's audible voice, but his words will ring clear when you need them. When faced with puzzling situations, appropriate Bible passages will pop into your mind. There is no end to the wisdom God can and will convey to you through Scripture as you nurture a personal relationship with him.

Chapter 8

Community: Hearing God Through Others

Moses' father-in-law replied, "What you are doing is not good. You and these people who come to you will only wear yourselves out. The work is too heavy for you; you cannot handle it alone."

—Exodus 18:17-18

"Time heals all wounds. Just give it time, and it'll get better." These were the words offered to Curtis by a well-intentioned co-worker, but they were not comforting or encouraging. Curtis was hurting. He had recently moved to take on a new job in a new town where he knew no one. Curtis was planning to propose to his girlfriend, who was still in college. But shortly after he moved, she dumped him, and he never saw it coming.

Job would have understood Curtis's pain. He had lost everything: his family, his livestock, his servants, his wealth, his entire livelihood. His friends Eliphaz, Bildad, and Zophar went to Job in his despair, but their words fell flat, and Job told them so. "I have heard many things like these; you are miserable comforters, all of you!" (Job 16:1).

Solicited and unsolicited advice that isn't God-centered can be confusing and damaging—especially when our emotions are raw. We look to others for help, but the pain we suffer often prevents us from properly assessing what we hear. Instead of feeling built up, we feel torn down. Weak instead of strong. Shameful instead of worthy. Like a failure.

That is how Curtis felt. He called himself a strong Christian, but because Curtis was new in town, he did not yet belong to a church that could help him navigate the depression that was setting in. As the pain deepened, Curtis began to contemplate suicide. In his desperate state, he cried out to God for help.

"Which of you fathers, if your son asks for a fish, will give him a snake instead? Or if he asks for an egg, will give him a scorpion? If you then, though you are evil, know how to give good gifts to your children, how much more will your Father in heaven give the Holy Spirit to those who ask him!" (Luke 11:11-13). When we ask for God's help, he answers. Our job is to remain diligent in seeking him.

God Provides

We are confronted with making choices every day. Some choices are instinctual. Some are calculated. We either respond without thinking or evaluate the data extensively before deciding. Curtis did both while leaning on God.

He went online and googled the attributes he desired in a church. Over and over, the name of one kept popping up. Curtis took this as a sign that God was leading him to this one church. He noted the times of the services and planned to attend that coming Sunday.

The large, white church sat back from the town's main street. Curtis parked his car, entered the building from the back, and sat down in the very last row of the sanctuary. Other worshippers came in and took their seats, but no one acknowledged Curtis's presence. It was as if he wasn't there.

The worship service opened with a children's choir that didn't resonate at all with Curtis. Then the pastor celebrated the accomplishment of an associate pastor. At this point, Curtis thought to himself, "There is nothing here for me." Out of respect, however, he stayed.

During the congregational songs and prayers, Curtis kept his eyes and ears open for any sign from God. But by the time the sermon rolled around, Curtis was wondering if he had misunderstood the signs and picked the wrong church.

Then the pastor read from the New Testament.

> That day when evening came, he said to his disciples, "Let us go over to the other side." Leaving the crowd behind, they took him along, just as he was, in the boat. There were also other boats with him. A furious squall came up, and the waves broke over the boat, so that it was nearly swamped. Jesus was in the stern, sleeping on a cushion. The disciples woke him and said to him, "Teacher, don't you care if we drown?"
>
> He got up, rebuked the wind and said to the waves, "Quiet! Be still!" Then the wind died down and it was completely calm.
>
> He said to his disciples, "Why are you so afraid? Do you still have no faith?"
>
> They were terrified and asked each other, "Who is this? Even the wind and the waves obey him!" (Mark 4:35-41)

Curtis recognized himself in the storm, and he silently asked God, "Don't you care that I'm perishing?"

The answer came straight from the pulpit when the pastor said something like this: "You may think you're in major trouble, in over your head. But Jesus is with you. You may think he doesn't see you, that he's asleep in the boat, but he sees everything. Ask him to calm the storm for you and to see you safely to the other side."

Occasionally a word is spoken without the speaker's knowledge of the role he plays in its delivery. But for the hearer who needs it, it is a divine message that opens the heart to healing. Curtis recognized God's voice in the pastor's words. It was the exact message he needed to hear. He was in the right place, after all.

"I don't know what would have happened to me if I hadn't gone to church that morning," Curtis said.

Week after week, Curtis returned to that large white church in the middle of town, and week after week, the pastor poured truth into him until Jesus came fully alive in his heart. About a year later, Curtis was attending church when his mother happened to tune in via livestream from her home in another state. She saw her son sitting in a row close to the front, and when the congregation stood to sing, she saw Curtis's hands rise in praise and worship. This, Curtis says, was a sign to her that God had fully healed her son.

God heard Curtis's cries for help and came to his rescue. In turn, Curtis recognized God's voice and was receptive to it. Today, Curtis is an active member of his church and is engaged to be married.

Used by God

There are times we don't recognize God's voice because pain, confusion, and stress are clouding our receptors. When our own spiritual eyes and ears aren't working properly, God will tap into other people to speak his truth into our struggles. While some of these people have no idea when they are being used as God's mouthpiece, others do.

When I was in the early stages of establishing myself as an author, I felt God nudge me to ask my readers to send me their prayer requests. They came pouring in. Some were vague; some were quite detailed. I printed them all and put them in a notebook where I could record God's responses as I prayed over each one.

Sheila had asked me to pray for her relationship with her daughter. I didn't have any other details, so I simply prayed that God would heal whatever was broken. As I prayed, I felt God say to me, "Sheila's daughter is angry about many things. She is hurting. She doesn't feel heard. Tell Sheila to validate her daughter. Just to acknowledge her."

To me, this directive sounded a little preachy, and I didn't know Sheila well enough to give her parenting advice, even if it came from God. Besides, I had promised to pray for people; I hadn't promised to provide insight.

But God didn't let me rest. He kept nudging me to reach out to Sheila. When I said my morning prayers, Sheila would pop into my head. When I saw a mother with her child, I'd get a feeling of angst. My stomach was in knots that were getting tighter. Though I couldn't see the point in sharing a discouraging word, I knew I had no right to question God's authority. "Consider carefully what you hear. With the measure you use, it will be measured to you—and even more" (Mark 4:24). God was calling me to speak truth, even if it made me uncomfortable.

I picked up the phone and made the call. I told Sheila as gently as possible that God wanted her to stop trying to fix the relationship and just love on her daughter. Sheila burst into tears. I wanted to crawl into a hole. But then Sheila said, "She's always saying to me, 'Stop talking! Just listen.' I really needed to hear what you told me! Thank you!"

What an honor it was for me to participate in this healing process! Looking back, I see I should never have hesitated to do what God told me to do, which was "Tell Sheila…." Withholding this valuable information was selfish and maybe a little prideful. It served as a reminder that God knows what each person needs, and it is a privilege to be used by him.

Trust and Obey

Gloria shared a similar story. Soon after they were married, she and her husband relocated to a new town. Because they knew no one, they immediately joined a church to make connections.

Gloria signed up for a women's Bible study, which was where she met Daisy. Both women were hoping to start families, but Daisy had recently miscarried and was told she could not bear children. Within months of each other, however, Gloria and Daisy became mothers—Gloria through natural childbirth and Daisy through adoption.

When Gloria became pregnant again, she was reluctant to tell Daisy. How could she rejoice in a second child when her dear friend was barren? Recalling what Jesus said to his disciples, "Whatever you ask for in prayer, believe that you have received it, and it will be yours" (Mark 11:24), Gloria got on her knees and prayed fervently.

After weeks of pleading on Daisy's behalf, Gloria heard God tell her to "trust and obey." She wasn't sure what that had to do with pregnancy, but she told God she was willing. The next thing Gloria heard rocked her world. "Daisy is with child. Tell her."

Really? Gloria desperately wanted to believe that what she heard was true, but how could she know for sure? What if the message hadn't come from God but was borne of her own deep desires? If she told Daisy what she believed God had said, would their friendship be ruined if it didn't come true? Gloria wrestled with this scenario, but each time she prayed, she heard, "Trust and obey."

I'd like to tell you that Gloria was obedient, but she wasn't. Instead of sharing the message God gave her, she continued to pray. Only now, she felt pressure on her chest as if her lungs were being compressed. The prophet Jeremiah had a similar experience when he wrote, "Sometimes I think, 'I will make no mention of his message. I will not speak as his messenger anymore.' But then his message becomes like a fire locked up inside of me, burning in my heart and soul. I grow weary of trying to hold it in; I cannot contain it" (Jeremiah 20:9 NET). Gloria's unpleasant feeling got stronger each day until, finally, she couldn't take it anymore.

"Daisy," she heard herself say, "you are such a special friend to me, and I need to share something with you. The Lord has pressed upon my heart to tell you that you are going to have a baby." The minute the words were out, Gloria felt the weight lift off her chest, and she could breathe with ease.

Daisy stared at Gloria in amazement. The announcement was not a surprise. Softly, Daisy admitted, "I'm pregnant." Fear of miscarriage had prevented her from sharing the news of her pregnancy with Gloria. But once the message was spoken and shared, both women rejoiced and rested in the promise of new life.

Gloria's encounter with God is a blessed reminder that prayer does work. "And when he speaks," Gloria adds, "we need to be obedient."

Many years have come and gone. Both women are the proud mothers of three children. Daisy even named her daughter after Gloria, a name that means eternal glory.

Listen to the Prophets

It is in God's nature to protect his people. Everything he says—or ever said—is for our own good. When our eyes and ears are not attuned to his frequency, however, we miss his life-giving words and follow a path of destruction. This is where prophets come in. God uses them to share his life-saving messages with those who are unable to hear him on their own.

With Babylon breathing down on Jerusalem, the king of Judah turned to the prophet Jeremiah for advice. Jeremiah told King Zedekiah, "If you surrender to the officers of the king of Babylon, your life will be spared and this city will not be burned down; you and your family will live. But if you will not surrender to the officers of the king of Babylon, this city will be given into the hands of the Babylonians and they will burn it down; you yourself will not escape from them" (Jeremiah 38:17-18).

This was not the advice Zedekiah was looking for. Instead of fearing God, he feared the Jews who had defected to Babylon. "They will not hand you over," Jeremiah assured him. "Obey the Lord by doing what I tell you. Then it will go well with you and your life will be spared" (Jeremiah 38:20). But Zedekiah didn't listen. He threw Jeremiah into prison. The result was disastrous. The king of Babylon broke through the walls of the holy city, slaughtered Zedekiah's sons in front of him, and then gouged out the king's eyes.

Zedekiah made a grave mistake when he asked for God's help and did not listen to the prophet who provided it. The outcome was death.

Let's compare this story to one that occurred 300 years earlier when King Jehoshaphat ruled Judah. He was a God-fearing man who took steps to abolish idol worship when he assumed the throne from his father. Despite his good heart—or maybe because of it—neighbors from the East waged war against him. When the king heard that a vast army was headed his way, he did not call in his advisors for advice. Instead, he stood before the people at the temple of the Lord and cried out to God.

> "Lord, the God of our ancestors, are you not the God who is in heaven? You rule over all the kingdoms of the nations. Power and might are in your hand, and no one can withstand you. Our God, did you not drive out the inhabitants of this land before your people Israel and give it forever to the descendants of Abraham your friend? They have lived in it and have built in it a sanctuary for your Name, saying, 'If calamity comes upon us, whether the sword of judgment, or plague or famine, we will stand in your presence before this temple that bears your Name and will cry out to you in our distress, and you will hear us and save us.'" (2 Chronicles 20:6-9)

Jehoshaphat's first line of defense was to publicly acknowledge God's authority over all things, speak of his power, and claim his promise of protection before the people of Judah. He demonstrated his trust in God by closing his appeal with these words: "We have no power to face this vast army that is attacking us. We do not know what to do, but our eyes are on you" (2 Chronicles 20:12). God responded through the words of Jahaziel, a priest and prophet who said, "Listen, King Jehoshaphat and all who live in Judah and Jerusalem! This is what the Lord says to you: 'Do not be afraid or discouraged because of this vast army. For the battle is not yours, but God's'" (2 Chronicles 20:15).

As king, Jehoshaphat could have dismissed Jahaziel's words, waiting instead for God to speak to him directly. But Jehoshaphat did not let his pride get in the way of wisdom. He accepted Jahaziel's message from God and "bowed down with his face to the ground, and all the people of Judah and Jerusalem fell down in worship before the Lord" (2 Chronicles 20:18).

Listen with Open Hearts

It is always easier to accept a prophetic message if it's positive, but positive doesn't always mean correct. "Do not believe every spirit, but test the spirits to see whether they are from God, because many false prophets have gone out into the world" (1 John 4:1). Remember, the devil knows Scripture and will twist it to use for his own evil purposes. Therefore, assess any spiritual messages you receive through a biblical lens to determine if they came from God.

To start, ask yourself if the messenger is someone who loves the Lord and lives according to his teachings. Is this a person you trust at the very core of your being? Only people who understand God's character and align their heart with his—like Jeremiah or Jahaziel—are entrusted with a prophetic message. If you don't know the messenger, however, don't write the message off just yet. God may use a random individual for a holy purpose. In such cases, listen carefully and judge the information by the content rather than the messenger.

Next, assess whether the message is scripturally sound. The words you hear should align with the Word of God and not worldly advice. For example, if someone tells you that God wants you to throw yourself off a bridge, don't believe him. There is nothing in the Bible that supports suicide, and God's messages will never contradict Scripture.

Finally, take the word you've received directly to God for clarity, and ask him whether the information is accurate. If discernment is not your gift, find someone who excels in this area. When we are too close to a painful situation, we usually can't correctly evaluate what we hear. Therefore, it is important to nurture Christian friendships alongside our relationship with the Lord.

While some people are called to deliver a message from God, others are called to respond to that message. Whichever role we play, we must be willing to listen with our hearts and respond with obedience.

GO DEEPER

The voices vying for our attention can be loud and confusing. It's even worse when we are in pain. People don't need advice when they are hurting; they need to be heard.

Practice listening well. When someone tells you a story, look them in the eye and ask questions that show interest instead of composing responses that are about you. For example, if a friend tells you a story about her dog, ask clarifying questions to learn more. Do not respond with a story about your own dog, your friend's dog, or why you don't like dogs. Enter the storyteller's world instead of forcing her into yours.

Later, when your friend experiences a painful or sorrowful situation, she will feel comfortable sharing with you because you have demonstrated that you know how to listen well. "Carry each other's burdens, and in this way you will fulfill the law of Christ" (Galatians 6:2).

Do not offer advice. Instead, pray with your friend and help her listen for God's word.

Likewise, listen carefully when someone offers you advice. Is this person someone you trust? If the answer is yes, take the advice to God in prayer for confirmation. "Trust in the Lord with all your heart and lean not on your own understanding; in all your ways submit to him and he will make your paths straight" (Proverbs 3:5-6).

If you have confirmed that the message you've received is from God, but you don't like it, remember what happened to Pharaoh when he refused to acknowledge the messages Moses shared. The Nile ran red with blood, crops were ruined, cattle died, and the life of his son—the heir to the Egyptian throne—was cut short. So, "Today, if you hear his voice [directly or through another person], do not harden your hearts" (Hebrews 4:7).

Chapter 9

Nature: God's Voice in Creation

The heavens declare the glory of God;
the skies proclaim the work of his hands.
Day after day they pour forth speech;
and night after night they reveal knowledge.

—Psalm 19:1-2

When I was 16, my family took a trip to the Grand Canyon. I had seen pictures of this geological wonder in books and was excited to travel across the country to see it in person. The most spectacular land feature I had seen to date was Niagara Falls, but because it was practically in my backyard, it no longer dazzled me. I hoped the canyon would thrill me the way the falls thrilled first-time visitors.

The landscape changed dramatically on the drive from upstate New York to Arizona, from Lake Erie to the Mississippi River to the Hoover Dam, from rolling hills to prairie lands to barren deserts, and from forests to farmland to canyon. The diversity was fascinating. It not only increased my interest in seeing the canyon, but it also testified to God's vast creativity.

As the sun began to set, Dad pulled the station wagon into one of those overview parking lots for our first glimpse of the Grand Canyon. Mom and I approached the railing together. With each step, more of the canyon came into view, yet the bottom managed to evade notice until we stood at the very edge of the precipice and leaned against the metal railing. I gasped. This was nothing like what I had imagined. Every stock photo had failed to capture the depth and breadth of this natural wonder; its magnitude was incomprehensible.

The shadows created by the clouds overhead danced among the rays of the setting sun and bounced off the distant stone walls. Both mesmerizing and paralyzing, the canyon's splendor paid homage to its magnificent creator. "Even before the mountains came into existence, or you brought the world into being, you were the eternal God" (Psalm 90:2 NET).

A tear rolled down my cheek. Then another. I glanced at my mom. She was crying, too. Before I knew it, we were holding each other and sobbing, overwhelmed by nature's glory. I had heard all about God's creativity, which was evident in the formation of the heavens and the earth. But, like Niagara Falls, the moon and stars were commonplace to me. They no longer astonished me when I looked into the night sky. But the Grand Canyon? Wow!

The words of the apostle Paul sum up the feelings I had that day. "For since the creation of the world, God's invisible qualities—his eternal power and divine nature—have been clearly seen, being understood from what has been made, so that people are without excuse" (Romans 1:20). Now I was without excuse as to the magnitude of God's splendor. His invisible qualities had been revealed to me as far as my eyes could see.

What We Take for Granted

It's easy to overlook the marvels of God's design when they occur regularly in our lives, especially when they can be explained by science. We know that the sun is the center of our universe and that Earth revolves around it. But back in the sixteenth century, the church convicted Galileo of heresy when he announced that the earth revolved around the sun. Who was man to contradict the words in the Bible?

And yet, if God truly gave humankind the gifts of intellect and reason, wouldn't he want us to discover all we could about creation and how it functions so that we could fully worship him as the ultimate creator of the universe? The more we learn about the world around us, the more we should be drawn to knowing God. Unfortunately, it doesn't always work that way.

When we put our faith in science alone, it diminishes our ability to understand the role humans were designed to play in caring for the planet. God gave us the earth to "subdue" and its creatures to "rule," but the divine benediction was issued under the premise that we would "be fruitful and increase in number" (Genesis 1:28). We were called to flourish for God's benefit, not our own. We were tasked with controlling the earth for the welfare of all, not exploiting its resources so a few could prosper.

Dr. Francis Collins, one of the world's leading scientists, was raised to respect others' beliefs but not from a Christian perspective. As a medical student, he considered himself an atheist, even though he recognized that religion comforted many of his patients.

In the early 1950s, the discovery of the double helix made headlines around the world as the template for the creation and operation of all living systems. Yet how it functioned was a mystery. Then Collins and his team at Yale University made a discovery in the deletion of three letters in the DNA code that led them to identify the cause of cystic fibrosis. This gave birth to the National Human Genome Research Institute, to which Collins was appointed to serve as its director. You might think that cracking the code that defines DNA and its chemical components would push a physician-geneticist further away from faith, but it did just the opposite.

Collins writes in his book *The Language of God*, "How aesthetically appealing and artistically sublime are the components of living things, from the ribosome that translates RNA into protein, to the metamorphosis of the caterpillar into the butterfly, to the fabulous plumage of the peacock attracting his mate! Evolution, as a mechanism, can be and must be true. But that says nothing about the nature of its author. For those who believe in

God, there are reasons now to be more in awe, not less."[16] Later, Collins would say that sequencing the human genome was "both a stunning achievement and an occasion of worship."[17]

The more Collins learned about the world around him, the more he recognized God as its creator. Science didn't squash his faith; science expanded it.

Know the Artist and the Art

I do not understand the biology of the human body, nor do I understand the depth of creativity behind a Mozart requiem or a Rodin sculpture. But this much I do know: To truly appreciate the significance of a creative work, we need to study the artist as well as his art. That said, if we want to know more about the universe, our planet, or ourselves, we need to learn more about God. The earth is God's work of art, and humankind is his masterpiece.

The Bible tells us several things about the creator of the universe. We know that he honors order because everything in creation has a purpose and a progression; nothing is random or disjointed. We also know he created everything out of nothing. "By faith we understand that the universe was formed at God's command, so that what is seen was not made out of what was visible" (Hebrews 11:3). And we know that every living creature is dependent on another living organism to survive. In summary, Earth and everything on it was designed by a master architect who left nothing to chance when he created something out of nothing.

Architect of the Universe

Cait is an intern architect. "Buildings are complex," she says. When designing one, architects think about how the structure will be used, by whom, how it will fit into the landscape, the budget, how long the structure should last, and how all the pieces (plumbing, electricity, walls, doors, etc.) fit together. According to Cait, the main thing they teach in architecture school is control. Cait admits she likes to be in control, so architecture was the perfect career path for her.

Cait threw herself into her studies and envisioned someday working in the community around her university. But then Hurricane Katrina hit and shut down her school in Louisiana. In response to the natural disaster, Cornell University in New York State offered online classes to students from Tulane. This budding architect took advantage of the opportunity by signing up for courses on landscape architecture.

Instead of learning how to control the environment, however, Cait was taught to respect it and utilize what nature provided. To help make the point, intricate French formal gardens were compared to English freeform gardens. The French style emphasized order and symmetry, while the English emphasized nature in its natural form. Both were beautiful to look at, and both took the same amount of effort to design, but only one was charming and inviting.

Cait was told she could design paths and walkways in the French style, but she could not expect people to stay on them. Instead of trying to change people's behavior, she was taught to utilize the English style in her designs, which encourages visitors to experience nature rather than view it from the sidelines.

Eventually, Cait graduated, got married, and moved to Hawaii, where she worked with an architectural firm that specialized in historic restoration. The island state was the perfect place for a nature-lover like Cait to live and work. When she became pregnant, her husband expressed a desire to start attending church. But because she was not a believer, Cait was uninterested. Nature was her god.

When her delivery date passed, Cait became anxious. To calm her nerves, she took a walk along Waimea Bay. It was September, and the waves were just beginning to swell as the weather transitioned from summer calm to winter spectacle. Cait found a peaceful place to sit down, high above the water, where she could take in the view for miles and meditate. As she stared at the vastness of the ocean, Cait suddenly became aware of the entire earth underneath her physical body and her connection to the whole world. "I felt the support of all nature on and in and of the earth. I felt connected to everything that existed and ever was alive. I felt a part of that!"

Through that one experience, Cait came to believe in a higher power. It was as if the switch to her faith was suddenly flipped on. God's omnipotent presence became known to Cait because he spoke to her in a language she would understand—architect to architect. Cait added, "I fully believed this force was a conscious creator who had a vision for the world."

A Vision for the World

We may not know God's exact plan for the world but rest assured, he has one, and all of nature is at his beck and call to achieve it. When God destroyed Sodom and Gomorrah, he rained down sulfur and fire. When the wickedness of humans increased, he flooded the whole earth. When he wanted to raise Joseph to a position of stature in Pharaoh's court, he initiated a seven-year famine. When God led his people out of bondage in Egypt, he parted the Red Sea. When Jesus died on the cross, the earth went dark for three hours. The list goes on, but the point is this: there is nothing in all of nature that God cannot wield to accomplish his purpose.

Whenever I hear of a flood or earthquake or any type of natural disaster, I can't help but wonder if it was just a force of nature or if God had a hand in it. God sees what we do not, and his plans are kingdom-driven. Therefore, it is quite possible that a disaster fulfills a heavenly purpose that is beyond our understanding, but it's also reasonable to assume that brokenness occurs naturally in a broken world. Whatever the case, God alone can bring something good out of a bad situation.

When I was six years old, my four-year-old brother was diagnosed with a rare form of cancer called Wilms Tumor. Over the course of two years, he underwent several surgeries and procedures as doctors attempted to eradicate the disease from his small body. Sadly, Jeff was not cured, and God called him home shortly after his sixth birthday.

Many years later, I took a job as a radio news reporter in the same city where my brother had been treated for his cancer. One morning, a press release crossed my desk announcing a breakthrough in the detection and treatment of Wilms Tumor. I immediately scheduled an interview with the lead doctor on the study, more for my benefit than for the radio listeners.

I was well-prepared for the interview, thanks to my mom, who helped me compile the questions I should ask. At the appointed time, I called the doctor, introduced myself as Michelle Layer (my maiden name), turned on my tape recorder with his permission, and began the interview. When it was over, the doctor asked me if I was a physician. I was honored that he thought so highly of my abilities, but I answered, "No. I am just familiar with this form of cancer because I had a brother who died from it many years ago."

There was a pause on the line. Then he asked, "Was his name Jeff?"

Shocked, I answered, "Yes! How did you know?"

This doctor knew the name of every child who had suffered from Wilms Tumor over the last 30 years as well as the treatments they had received. When I introduced myself at the start of the interview, the doctor noticed I had the same last name as one of the children in the study. I came to learn that my mother had signed numerous consent forms that allowed doctors to perform a variety of experimental procedures on Jeff in the hopes of finding a cure.

"Is your mother still alive?" this doctor asked me.

"Yes," I answered.

"Please tell her, 'Thank you.' Without parents like her, this breakthrough would not have been possible. Many children will survive this form of cancer because of her actions."

Today, the survival rate of Wilms Tumor patients is more than 80 percent. Back in 1971, when Jeff died, less than 40 percent of children lived more than four years.

I can't say that my mother was comforted by the fact that others would live because her son had died. Nor do I know why God allowed Jeff to suffer so much in his short life. But this much I do know: God can take painful situations and use them for good. He sees things differently than we do. He sees the big picture when we are focused on the details. He sees the world—both the past and the future—from a perspective we cannot begin to comprehend. "For my thoughts are not your thoughts, neither are your ways my ways," declares the Lord. "As the heavens are higher than the earth, so are my ways higher than your ways and my thoughts than your thoughts" (Isaiah 55:8-9).

God's Purposeful Design

When dark clouds roll in, we know a storm is coming. When the ice starts to melt, we know spring is on its way. Certain flowers, like daisies and poppies, close their petals in advance of rain, and certain animals, like cows and sheep, become agitated and huddle together prior to bad weather.

God provided us with a world that reflects order as he designed it, where man, animals, and nature work in perfect harmony. Even a forest fire, which devastates the landscape, has its advantages. As underbrush and dead leaves are burned away, nutrients are returned to the soil. This allows the roots of established trees to grow stronger. There are even certain plant species that rely on fire to help them release their seeds so they can propagate. God could have made the trees all the same color and height, perfectly symmetrical. But he didn't. Each one is unique and serves a different purpose—just like us. As my architect friend Cait says, "Nothing God created is by accident. Everything he designed was thoughtful and intentional."

Nothing humans design is by accident either. However, because our sights are limited, we attempt to control our surroundings rather than use the knowledge God gave us to adapt to them.

> But now, ask the animals and they will teach you,
> or the birds of the sky and they will tell you.
> Or speak to the earth and it will teach you,
> or let the fish of the sea declare to you.
> Which of all these does not know
> that the hand of the Lord has done this?
> In his hand is the life of every creature
> and the breath of all the human race. (Job 12:7-10 NET)

Examine the world from an architect's point of view: the design, the color, the form, and the function—from the majestic mountains to the rolling valleys, from pink sunrises to orange sunsets, from blooming flowers to towering trees, from Niagara Falls to the Grand Canyon—all are intentional works of art created by the master artist for our pleasure and his glory.

But out of all God's grand designs, we alone were created like him. "God created humankind in his own image, in the image of God he created them, male and female he created them" (Genesis 1:27 NET). God has planted his seed of creativity in each one of us, a seed that begs to be nurtured and cultivated. Are you aware of your unique design and function, and are you using your gifts to glorify your creator? All of nature echoes God's power and majesty, and so must we.

GO DEEPER

Why would a perfect God design an imperfect world? He wouldn't, and he didn't. There is a plan and a purpose for every piece of creation, and we all fit together like the pieces of a galactic puzzle.

John Muir, one of our country's most influential conservationists, once said, "In every walk with nature, one receives far more than he seeks." Take a walk outside and marvel at the variety of flora and fauna. Select one tree or plant and examine it closely. What are its strengths? What are its weaknesses? How does it relate to the land around it? Does it contain any fruit, nuts, or flowers? Who or what benefits from this tree or plant? Why did God create it? How would the landscape feel if it was covered with just this one type of tree or plant?

Stand in awe of God as the master architect and praise him in wonder and glory. "Oh Lord, what a variety of things you have made! In wisdom you have made them all. The earth is full of your creatures" (Psalm 104:24 NLT).

God created us to care for the earth and its inhabitants. "The Lord is good to all; he has compassion on all he has made" (Psalm 145:9). In the United States alone, each year, more than 60 million tons of air pollution is emitted into the atmosphere, and more than 260 million tons of waste is produced with half going into landfills. The situation is even worse in other countries. Do you have compassion toward God's creation? What have you taken for granted, abused, or ignored? What could you do differently to demonstrate concern for the earth now and for future generations? You may think your small changes can't make a difference, but great things happen one step at a time.

Chapter 10

Time: God's Control of Each Moment

He has made everything beautiful in its time.
He has also set eternity in the human heart;
yet no one can fathom what God has done from beginning to end.

—Ecclesiastes 3:11

The alarm rang at the fire station just after 2:00 a.m. In less than a minute, the veteran crew was up, dressed, and rolling toward a burning home in eastern Wisconsin. Despite the sleet, it was business as usual. On route, the dispatcher alerted the firefighters to the situation: two children were trapped in the basement of a burning house. Basement fires were especially hard to fight because the smoke and heat had nowhere to go except up the stairwell. With the escape route concealed by smoke, this would no longer be just a fight against fire; it would be a search and rescue.

The engine company's captain had spent his entire career battling blazes on the north side of Milwaukee. Responding to calls ran like clockwork, but extra urgency kicked in when kids were involved. Every bit of adrenaline was used to focus on recovery, and split-second decisions resulted in life or death.

When Engine 24 turned onto North 67th Street, Greg and his team were immediately shrouded in smoke. Not only was it impossible to see the house numbers, but it was also impossible to determine which house was on fire. The driver slowed the engine. "Boss," he said, "the house has to be right around here."

Suddenly a woman appeared out of the smoke, screaming in fear. "There are two boys trapped in the basement. Please don't let them die!"

While the crew loaded hose on their backs, Greg followed the woman to the back of the house. His stomach clenched. The smoke emerging from the stairwell was black and, therefore, combustible. If provided with enough heat and oxygen, the smoke would ignite in a flashover. Greg knew he was entering a toxic atmosphere where survival was slim.

"Please don't let them die," the woman screamed. "They were calling for help right before you got here!"

Greg was encouraged to know that the boys had recently been alert, but time was running out. There are two rules every firefighter lives by: never enter a building alone, and don't walk into a fire without a charged hose line for protection. Greg ignored both. He leapt down the stairs, risking his own life to save the kids.

When he hit the bottom of the stairs, Greg fell to his knees. Crawling into a room on all fours was standard practice in a space with zero visibility. Through his mask, he called out, "Are you guys down here?" There was no response, only the sound of fire crackling off to his right.

With approximately fifteen minutes' worth of air in his tank, Greg crawled into the room. His left hand maintained contact with the floor while his right hand swept the area in front of him. Suddenly his hand hit a stationary object. A bed. Knowing children often crawl under beds to hide from smoke, Greg felt underneath. No one was there. He flipped the mattress. Still no one. Inching his way around the bed's perimeter, Greg came upon a pile of bedding. He systematically tore into the layers. His hands landed on what felt like a large rag doll, limp and lifeless.

The sound of more firefighters alerted Greg to crawl back to the stairwell, where he turned the body over to a crew member. Then he dove back into the smoke to feel for the other child. Moments later, Greg located the second boy. He, too, was limp and lifeless.

Greg was certain that both boys were dead. He had done his job, and he had done it well. But no amount of experience could have saved those children. This was something Greg did not have time to think about. He had a fire to fight.

Forty minutes later, the fire was out, and the walls had been ripped open to ensure nothing was smoldering within. Greg could now see clearly what had been invisible upon arrival. There was no reason to stay in the basement any longer, but Greg had no desire to go outside, where he was sure to see two small bodies covered by yellow sheets.

Slowly, Greg ascended the stairs. The smoke had dissipated, and he scanned the landscape.

"Amazing job, Engine twenty-four!" the battalion chief exclaimed. "Both boys have been resuscitated on scene and are on their way to the hospital."

Greg heard the news, but his logical brain could not accept this illogical outcome.

Time Stands Still

Have you ever felt like time had stopped? Like you were moving in slow motion, or everything around you had slowed to a standstill? In such an atmosphere, miracles happen.

Hezekiah was one of the rare Judean kings who sought to abolish idol worship and remain faithful to the God of his ancestors. When Israel fell to Assyria, Hezekiah prayed for deliverance, and God put 185,000 Assyrian soldiers to death while they slept.

One day, Hezekiah became deathly ill, and the prophet Isaiah came to him with a message from the Lord. "Set your affairs in order, for you are going to die. You will not recover from this illness" (2 Kings 20:1 NLT).

When Hezekiah heard this, he called out to God to remember his faithfulness and spare his life. God evidently honored Hezekiah's prayer because Isaiah returned moments later with a new word from the Lord. Not only was God going to heal Hezekiah, but he was also going to add fifteen years to his life.

King Hezekiah was skeptical about this new report and asked for a sign.

> Isaiah replied, "This is your sign from the Lord confirming that the Lord will do as he has said. Do you want the shadow to move ahead ten steps or go back ten steps?" Hezekiah answered, "It is easy for the shadow to lengthen ten steps, but not for it to go back ten steps." Isaiah the prophet called out to the Lord, and the Lord made the shadow go back ten steps on the stairs of Ahaz. (2 Kings 20:9-11 NET)

If God could alter the movement of the sun and add years to a man's life, he could surely stop time to allow an engine company to save the lives of two boys. Our God is not confined by time as we know it. "Now, dear friends, do not let this one thing escape your notice, that a single day is like a thousand years with the Lord and a thousand years are like a single day" (2 Peter 3:8 NET).

Protocol calls for fire battalions to log the time of each run. This means that the time of each step is recorded—when the alarm sounds, when the engine pulls out of the station, when the truck arrives on the scene, when firefighters enter the site, when victims are pulled from a burning building, and so on. Greg examined the fire report when he got back to the station and struggled to make sense of what he was seeing. From the time firefighters arrived on the scene until the boys were out of the basement, less than two minutes had passed. That was impossible. Finding occupants in blinding smoke takes time—certainly more than two minutes. It didn't make sense. Either the times were recorded incorrectly or God had intervened.

Slowing

Many of us scurry through life like a squirrel on amphetamines. We rise early and go to bed late. We apply makeup while driving, eat at our desks, and text in snippets. We attempt to do several things at once and do nothing well. That's because multitasking is a myth. God did not create our brains to address two activities at the same time. What we consider multitasking is our brain volleying rapidly between tasks. The more activities we add to the mix, the less efficient we become and the more likely we are to make mistakes.

In our fast-paced world, where desires can be filled within hours or minutes, patience is rare, and expediency is a virtue. The more we have, the more we want, and the quicker we want it. Rarely satisfied with the way things are, we fill the emptiness we feel inside with more things, more activities, and more interactions. This vortex builds speed and sucks us further and further into the abyss, from which it becomes harder and harder to emerge.

We can learn from the apostle Paul who wrote, "I have learned to be content whatever the circumstances. I know what it is to be in need, and I know what it is to have plenty. I have learned the secret of being content in any and every situation, whether well-fed or hungry, whether living in plenty or in want. I can do all this through him who gives me strength" (Philippians 4:11-13).

Take a look at your own life. Are you content? As you move through each day, do you speed up or slow down? We can learn a lot from Jesus, who moved intentionally and purposely as he focused on one task at a time, one person at a time. We all know how it feels to be in conversation with someone who is distracted by their phone. We feel unheard, unimportant, and unworthy. These are not feelings Jesus would have wanted people to feel, nor should we.

Slowing down comes with health benefits. It can relieve stress, reduce anxiety, improve cognition, increase creativity, and strengthen patience. It also helps us be more grateful, more content, and more observant. When God created the Sabbath, it was to ensure that we would have time to enjoy downtime with him.

If your hope is to notice God more often, you will need to slow down and consciously direct your mind to be more attentive to the present moment and God's presence in it.

Time for God

God rarely seems to be in a hurry. Maybe it's because he has all the time in the world, or maybe it's because he is giving us time to process our sanctification.

For forty years following their exodus from Egypt, God had the Israelites wander in the desert. That's how long it took for a new generation to come into adulthood—people who knew only of God's leadership and little of the country their parents left behind. Though Moses was able to take God's people out of Egypt, he couldn't take Egypt out of the people. Only time could accomplish that.

Transformation takes time. Yet, in these times, time is scarce and hard to find. But let's get one thing straight: time cannot be found. It must be reserved. Like Jesus, we must be intentional about setting time aside to communicate with our Father in heaven.

Tom, a commercial airline pilot and committed Christian, was stuck in a pattern of worry and stress. He noticed himself rushing through his prayers so he could attend to the tasks of the day. This only made him more tense, which emerged as frustration and anger. Unable to calm his mind, Tom realized he needed more than a vacation. More than a retreat. He needed a reset.

Would twenty days in the wilderness be enough to cleanse his mind and reboot his heart? This is what Tom wondered. After much prayer, he settled on forty days because of its Biblical significance.

Planning and executing a forty-day escape from civilization is no easy feat, but Tom did it. A friend drove him and his forty-day supply of food to the Deep Creek Mountains of western Utah, where Tom hid three-quarters of his food supply behind some trees and loaded the remaining items into his backpack. Bidding his friend goodbye, he hiked several miles into the woods, where he set up camp near a running stream. That night, Tom paraphrased Romans 12:2 in his journal.

> I'm rejoicing in the hope of the transformation that will take place, praying to not conform any longer to the pattern of this world, but to be transformed by the renewing of my mind—to know God's perfect will, and to carry it out.

Tom began a routine of reading the Bible, praying, meditating, journaling, and hiking each day. Twelve days in, Tom wrote that he was overwhelmed by the number of days remaining.

> What's wrong with me? Why am I wishing the time and days away? Why am I counting the days to 40? Why am I trying to speed up time? I know you are doing a work in me. I know that work is just beginning and because of my restlessness it will take time. I don't want to return home until your work is done. I don't want to return home unchanged. Be patient with me, Lord. Help me to be in the moment. Help me to be in today and not worry about the days ahead.

The very next day, Tom started to calm down. He wrote, "It seems perhaps the entire 40 days will be needed to help me return with a renewed mind."

As his desire to stay busy diminished, his conviction to honor the Sabbath increased. There were other changes as well. His sense of hearing, smell, and taste became more acute as Tom assimilated into his surroundings. His instincts sharpened, too. By day seventeen, Tom's anxiety waned. He became more attuned to the work God was doing in him, and his prayer life took a turn as requests for comfort and well-being shifted to prayers for strength and equipping. When an unexpected snow and blustery wind froze his drinking water and snuffed out his fire, Tom prayed for fortitude. He journaled that he believed God had a purpose in isolating him in his tent until the bad weather passed.

After forty-eight hours, the sun finally appeared, and the tone of Tom's journal entries changed.

> What a blessing!! The sun is shining. It feels SO GOOD! No wind, clear blue skies, the snow is melting, the ground is thawing. My spirits are lifted. I'm encouraged. Praise God! There is a lesson to be learned here, I believe. It is patience in affliction, as Romans 12:12 states. "Suffering produces perseverance, perseverance character, and character hope—and hope does not put us to shame because God's love has been poured out into our hearts through the Holy Spirit who has been given to us" (Romans 5:3-5). Wow!

On day twenty-five, Tom was no longer worried about the days ahead. Instead, he was content to be still in God's presence. Just God and him, hanging out at the campfire, conversing about spiritual things, and enjoying each other's company. Tom wrote, "I stayed up later than usual, kept adding wood to the fire, and enjoying the time."

The next two weeks proved to be critical in Tom's journey. He fell into a routine with God, whom he recognized as his constant companion. There were times, Tom says, that he felt the tangible presence of another person in his tent. Fear subsided as peace, acceptance, and gratitude took root.

The last three days of Tom's forty-day journey into the wilderness were the most transformative.

> I've found during this journey that when I have more time than I know what to do with, my prayers are deeper and longer, and that the Holy Spirit guides them. Rather than rush through prayer, I desire to lengthen them, to stay in prayer as long as possible so the Holy Spirit guides my thoughts and words. This is not possible when there are timelines and agendas that need attending.

Tom's return to the real world went smoothly, and years later, his transformation hasn't waned. He is calmer, more patient, and moves through life at a slower pace, no longer trying to cram more activities into a day than humanly possible. The Sabbath has become something Tom diligently honors with worship, rest, and time with God. "The more time we spend uninterrupted with God, the better life is," Tom says. "It's not that life gets any easier or that life's challenges dissipate, but it's that we see life and its challenges from a different perspective, one that permits peace even amid turmoil—a perspective that replaces fear with faith, hope, trust."

Time's Purpose

God created time with limits that humankind stretched. We have calendars and schedules, dates and agendas, vacations and sabbaticals, times to beat, and times to get away. We waste time, spend time, pass time, and lose time. We say, "All in God's timing," but then we move ahead and set our own time. Yet, when we surrender to God's time, we step into a spiritual flow that carries us along like a leaf on a gentle stream.

I have found that intentional quality time with God can make even the most stressful days more manageable. When there are too many things on my plate, quiet time with the Lord in prayer paves a calm route forward. Logically, this doesn't make sense. Shouldn't I work faster, harder, or more efficiently? That's what our culture would prescribe. But God—who controls time, bends time, lengthens it and shortens it, even makes it disappear—creates a way where there doesn't appear to be a way. I have sometimes marveled at how much I was able to accomplish after spending extended time with God. How was that possible? "Come near to God, and he will come near to you" (James 4:8).

Barbara L. Peacock, a spiritual director and author, says that "life sucks up the moisture of our souls if we don't replenish daily and often."[18] It is imperative that we make time to be with God, for he alone can refill our spirits and transform us into the women and men he designed us to be.

GO DEEPER

The fourth commandment states, "Remember the Sabbath day by keeping it holy. Six days you shall labor and do all your work, but the seventh day is a sabbath to the Lord your God. On it you shall not do any work, neither you, nor your son or daughter, nor your male or female servant, nor your animals, nor any foreigner residing in your towns" (Exodus 20:8-10). God himself modeled Sabbath behavior for us at creation when he rested on the seventh day.

In the same way that we were not created for multitasking, we were not created to work without rest. There is only so much we can endure, and studies prove that to function well, our bodies need a break. Our brains need rest, too. So do our immune systems. Our hearts need it, and our souls need it. This is why Jesus said, "The Sabbath was made for people, and not people for the Sabbath" (Mark 2:27 NET). Rest is necessary—not only to improve our health but also to strengthen our relationship with God.

Select a twenty-four-hour period to unplug. It doesn't have to be a Sunday—any day of the week is fine. During this time, stay off the computer and away from social media and the news. Read. Bake cookies. Journal. Create art. Take a walk. Work on a puzzle. Light a candle and read your Bible. As you move slowly (yes, slowly) through your day, acknowledge God's presence in everything you do. Speak to him and thank him. Keep the hours holy.

If you have children, endeavor to make the Sabbath family time. Have everyone turn off their electronics and place them in a Sabbath basket for the day or just for a few hours. Discuss what you will do together and alone. For this to work well, students should complete their homework before the start of Sabbath so they, too, can enjoy this holy time.

In addition to a weekly Sabbath day, carve out time daily to pause with God. You might set an alarm to remind yourself to take a break. Slow down. Smell the roses. Enjoy a sunrise or sunset. After a month, evaluate any differences you notice in your temperament, body, or relationships. Then ask yourself, can you afford not to slow down and keep the Sabbath as God designed?

Chapter 11

The Word: Seeking God in Scripture

All Scripture is God-breathed and is useful
for teaching, rebuking, correcting and training in righteousness,
so that the servant of God may be thoroughly equipped for every good work.

—2 Timothy 3:16-17

FINALLY, a chapter that addresses hearing God's voice through Scripture. Even though the importance of Scripture has been woven throughout this book, reading the Bible now gets a chapter of its own—near the end, where it has the best chance of making a lasting impression.

Like a good set of bookends, Scripture holds up our relationship with God and prevents everything in between from falling down. It is the structure that frames our lives and keeps us walking the path of God's righteousness. The Bible is God's story, our history, and a guidebook on how life is supposed to be lived with, in, and through Christ. Everything we really need to know is contained within its pages.

Asking the Right Questions

"What about dinosaurs?"

That was the question one of the students at our youth retreat asked our seasoned speaker. His response was curious. "What about them?"

"Did they exist?" the student asked. "The Bible doesn't say anything about dinosaurs."

Many people question the authority of the Bible because it doesn't contain a complete history of the earth. Others read the Bible literally and take it as law. Both extremes miss the point. The Bible is not a book about the creation of the world, nor is it the statutes of the heavenly realm. The Bible is a love story. It is meant to be read with our hearts. "It requires more faith, effort, prayer, humility, vulnerability, and often time to read God's word with our hearts, but that's because the heart is precisely where God wants his word to land."[19]

So, what about the dinosaurs?

They have nothing to do with love. Therefore, you won't find them in the Bible. If you want to know about dinosaurs, turn to science. If you want to know about God's love for us, turn to Scripture.

Loving God with Your Heart

I was a bit of a party girl in my former life and, I'm sad to say, a hypocrite. I went to church every Sunday, but most evenings, I could be found partying, drinking, and looking for love in all the wrong places. Consistent church attendance did not make me a Christian. Had you asked me back then what God wanted of me, I likely would have said, "To be a good person."

I had no idea what God wanted. I wasn't even close.

King David is called "a man after God's own heart" (1 Samuel 13:14) even though he committed adultery, sent an innocent man to his death, and lied to save his own skin. Given these behaviors, why was this sinful man bestowed with such an enduring legacy? The answer is quite simple. He loved God. King David demonstrated his love for the Lord by striving to keep God's requirements, his decrees, his laws, and his commands. When David failed, he was quick to repent, praise God in holiness, trust in his promises, and recommit his life to following the Lord. David put his heart into his personal relationship with God, and that made all the difference.

As a young adult, I had no relationship with the Lord. My knowledge of the Bible was limited to the big stories, like Moses' parting of the Red Sea, Jonah and the whale, Joseph and his coat of many colors, and Christ's crucifixion. I knew *about* God, but I didn't *know* God. That started to change when my marriage fell apart.

For reasons I am still unable to explain (except by the Holy Spirit), my first desire after separating from my husband was to get to know God personally. This led me to enroll in a year-long Bible study. Thankfully, my older brother had given me a Bible years earlier. It was gathering dust on my bookshelf and begging to be used.

The instructor, Mike, was a joyful man who could quote Scripture with ease. The hefty homework he assigned was intended to saturate us in the Word, and it did! Under his tutelage, I came to see that the books of the Bible were all connected—just one big love story that pointed to the Messiah. Even the books in the Old Testament foretold his coming.

"Mike," I asked, "why have I never noticed this before?"

He answered simply. "Were you looking?"

For forty years, I had been ignorantly complacent in my faith, satisfied with what little I knew—or what I thought I knew. I did not seek anything more than what I had been spoon-fed on Sunday mornings. As a result, God was living on the periphery of my mind and nowhere in my heart.

When an expert in religious law asked Jesus to name the most important commandment, "Jesus replied, 'Love the Lord your God with all your heart and with all your soul and with all your mind'" (Matthew 22:37). Notice that he said to love with our hearts first and our minds last. This is because God wants a relationship with each one of us, and you can't have a relationship if your heart isn't in it.

Remember

"God demonstrates his own love for us in this: while we were still sinners, Christ died for us" (Romans 5:7-8). Try to grasp the significance of that statement. Before we committed one sin, Jesus paid the penalty. He knew we would mess up, and he willingly took the blame. He went beyond covering us with liability insurance; he bought the company. That is a crazy, unfathomable, ridiculous, outrageous, and unbelievable kind of love! One that should not be taken for granted but often is.

Our memory is selective. We best remember the things we intentionally focus on (e.g., studying for a test) or situations that elicit a feeling (e.g., a first date). Our strongest memories are connected to our strongest emotions, which range from joy to pain. But it's hard to remember stories in which we played no active role, stories that were passed down from our ancestors. This is because they live in our heads and not in our hearts. Yet, remembering is exactly what God asks us to do.

"Remember that you were slaves in Egypt and that the LORD your God brought you out of there with a mighty hand and an outstretched arm" (Deuteronomy 5:15). "Remember well what the Lord your God did to Pharaoh and to all Egypt" (Deuteronomy 7:18). "Be careful that you do not forget the Lord your God, failing to observe his commands, his laws and his decrees" (Deuteronomy 8:11). "Remember the Lord your God, for it is he who gives you the ability to produce wealth, and so confirms his covenant, which he swore to your ancestors, as it is today" (Deuteronomy 8:18).

When we forget all that God has done for us, that we are meant to be in a relationship with our creator, that there is a divine plan for our lives, and most of all, when we forget what God told us to remember, we enter a course headed for disaster.

Do you remember what happened to King Solomon's kingdom? Let me remind you.

Solomon assumed the reign of Israel when his father, King David, died. Instead of following God's commands with his heart as his father had, Solomon allowed foreign gods to enter Israel as a means to secure peace with his neighbors. Though he is remembered as a wise king, his actions led to Israel's schism. While Solomon was still on the throne, God set into motion a series of events that would eventually split the kingdom in two: the northern kingdom of Israel with ten tribes and the southern kingdom of Judah with two tribes. God does not take idol worship lightly. Remember the first commandment (and it's first for a reason!): "You shall have no other gods before me" (Exodus 20:3).

Idol worship was still prevalent in Judah when King Josiah took the throne some 300 years later. In the eighteenth year of his reign, the king ordered repairs to be made to the temple in Jerusalem. In the process, the high priest discovered the Book of the Law. The holy scroll had apparently been misplaced—perhaps for centuries—and no one missed it. However, when it was found, it was appropriately presented to the king for review.

When Josiah heard the words of the scroll, he tore his robes and said, "Go and inquire of the Lord for me and for the people and for all Judah about what is written in this book that has been found. Great is the Lord's anger that burns against us because those who have gone before us have not obeyed the words of this book; they have not acted in accordance with all that is written there concerning us" (2 Kings 22:13).

Josiah took the words of the Lord to heart, and God noticed. He was allowed to reign and die in peace. Disaster would still come to Judah, but Josiah would not have to witness it.

From Your Head to Your Heart

"My child, do not forget my teaching, but let your heart keep my commandments" (Proverbs 3:1 NET). Over and over throughout the Bible, God emphasizes the importance of remembering him with our hearts (not our heads) and passing our memories on to the next generation where they can dwell in their hearts (not in their heads). It is impossible to do this, however, unless we get to know Jesus personally.

We begin by reading the Bible for knowledge. This is where it starts. But over time, as we come to remember the stories and activate God's word in our lives, we will discover that we are no longer reading for knowledge alone. We have moved to reading the Bible for relationship. "If we wish to understand God's personal relationship to us, including how he speaks to us individually today, we must understand what the word of God is in general and how both the Son of God and the Bible are the Word of God."[20]

Donna was part of a study group whose members met once a week for the sole purpose of deepening their faith. They read scholarly books together, studied the Bible, and practiced various spiritual disciplines. The curriculum was head centered, but it was designed to saturate the brain and overflow into the heart.

One morning, Donna sat down to practice contemplative prayer, which is also called imaginative prayer. She opened her Bible to the Gospel of Mark and chose a passage that dealt with healing. Planting her feet firmly on the floor and her hands—palms up—on her thighs, she closed her eyes and breathed slowly. In her mind's eye, Donna imagined herself in the story. She took note of her surroundings, inhaled the smells, and looked for Jesus in the crowd. By now, she knew him well enough to recognize him if he appeared.

Suddenly, it all became real.

Donna had not been praying for Jesus to show her the reality of Scripture, but he responded in 3D. What she remembers most clearly is not how things looked but how she felt. She sensed someone taking hold of her hands as she was washed in peace, warmth, and love. "He spoke to me," Donna said, "but not in words."

This is the power of Scripture in action. It is not dead or irrelevant. "For the word of God is alive and active. Sharper than any double-edged sword, it penetrates even to dividing soul and spirit, joints and marrow; it judges the thoughts and attitudes of the heart" (Hebrews 4:12).

I cannot stress the importance of allowing Scripture to move from your head to your heart. If it remains in your head, you run the risk of viewing Scripture as holy law. But if you learn to read it from your heart, you will recognize it as the love letter it is.

Jesus was accused multiple times of breaking the law because he healed on the Sabbath, but nowhere in the Bible does it specifically state that healing someone on this holy day is wrong. What the Bible does say is, "The seventh day is a Sabbath day of rest dedicated to the Lord your God. On that day no one in your household may do any work" (Exodus 20:10 NLT). In their wisdom, Jewish religious leaders came to define what constituted work, and somewhere along the way, healing was identified.

Jesus said to the Jewish leaders who were harassing him for healing on the Sabbath, "You search the Scriptures because you think they give you eternal life. But the Scriptures point to me!" (John 5:39 NLT).

So, why do we read the Bible? Not to understand the law. Not to discover hidden meanings. Not because we have to. We read the Bible to find Jesus.

Seek Him in the Word

The Lord said, "I love those who love me, and those who seek me find me" (Proverbs 8:17). If we pray with love and seek God with our hearts, chances are he will answer in extraordinary—even phenomenal—ways.

Grace majored in political science at a prestigious university, but she secretly aspired to become a songwriter and recording artist. During her sophomore year, shortly after posting her first song on social media, she took a class on critical race theory. Grace became riled by what she was learning, often leaving class feeling deeply unhappy. Back in her apartment, the sweet love songs she had been writing morphed into resistance songs loaded with angry lyrics. By the end of that semester, Grace had written around twenty tunes that addressed social issues plaguing the black community. She recorded several and posted a few on TikTok.

Initially, Grace's songs weren't getting much traction, but that was about to change. First, the world started shutting down due to the COVID-19 pandemic. Then George Floyd's murder by a police officer was caught on camera, and protests erupted across the country. Against a backdrop of police brutality, Joseph Biden won the presidential election, which spurred a mob of disillusioned voters to attack the U.S. Capitol. It was the perfect storm. People were angry, and Grace's music resonated with them.

When one of her songs went viral, Grace decided it was time to make an album. But here's what you need to know: Grace is a mature Christian. She loves the Lord and seeks his guidance in all things. She was only going to move forward with this musical project if God was on board.

Grace sat cross-legged on the couch at her mother's house. With her songwriting journal on one leg and her Bible on the other, she prayed that God would make his desires clear to her. Would he support putting the resistance songs she had written out into the world, of which several could be deemed radical?

Internal conflicts are commonplace for Christians. The apostle Paul struggled with his flesh and wrote, "I love God's law with all my heart. But there is another power within me that is at war with my mind. This power makes me a slave to the sin that is still within me" (Romans 7:22-23 NLT). Martin Luther struggled to please God through his pious actions before realizing that God wanted his heart. Saint John of the Cross struggled whenever he felt the absence of God's presence. He called this "the dark night of the soul." And now Grace was struggling. Something inside told her it wouldn't be good to release all those angry songs into the world, but she wanted to hear that answer directly from God.

As she sat praying, her internal thoughts fluctuated. "Talk to me, God," she pleaded. Then she would sit quietly and listen. As time passed, Grace spoke a line from the prophet Samuel, "Speak Lord, your servant is listening" (1 Samuel 3:9). She repeated this line several times with growing intensity. Still, nothing.

Grace did not doubt that God had heard her. Though she couldn't feel him, she knew he was there. Grace expected an answer, but she also knew she couldn't force God to speak. Frustrated and at the end of her patience, she decided to make her request specific. "Look, God, I am going to open my Bible randomly, and I am going to take the first sentence I see as your answer."

This is not something Grace (or I) would normally do or recommend. But Grace rationalized her decision because she had been wrestling with God for a while and was holding her appeal loosely. If the passage she found had nothing to do with her situation, she would still honor God as Lord of her life. Grace reconciled, however, that because Scripture provides a direct route to connecting with God, it was the perfect means of communication if the Holy Spirit was willing to respond.

Grace closed her eyes and placed her hand on the Bible. Slipping her fingers between the pages, she flipped the book open. Her eyes landed on Psalm 101.

> I will sing of your love and justice, Lord.
> I will praise you with songs.
> I will be careful to live a blameless life—when will you come to help me?
> I will lead a life of integrity in my own home.
> (Psalm 101:1-2 NLT)

For Grace, the answer was immediately clear. If she wanted God's blessing, she needed to sing songs of love and justice that did not point a finger at who was to blame. She was to rise above the prejudice and practice mercy.

Of the twelve songs Grace had planned to put on her first album, only five made the cut as written. The others had to be revised or written from scratch. Grace entitled her album *Love and Justice.**

The Power of the Word

Scripture is as relevant today as ever. Each time I reread a passage, I acquire new insight and clarity. I don't know how this works, but it does. From Genesis to Revelation, every word in the Bible is important, and every word is powerful. The more we study it, the more we know about God. The more we know about God, the better our chances of developing a relationship with him. And the deeper our relationship gets with our creator, the more adept we will become at recognizing his presence. "After he has gathered his own flock, he walks ahead of them, and they follow him because they know his voice" (John 10:4 NLT).

So, immerse yourself in the Bible. Learn the Scriptures well and live them well. Once you get into the Word, the Word will get into you.

---

* *Love and Justice* came out in early 2022. To date, the album has had roughly 4 million streams industrywide and contains "Down in Virginia," the song that first went viral. Grace Victoria's music can be purchased online wherever music is sold.

GO DEEPER

"While deep experiences of the presence and power of God can happen in innumerable ways, the ordinary way of going deeper spiritually into prayer is through meditation on Scripture."[21] Meditating on Scripture can help to nurture your relationship with Christ by moving the word from your head into your heart.

Select a Bible reading for meditation that focuses on God's character. Here are several passages you might consider that all address his unconditional love for us.

- Psalm 36:5-10
- John 3:16-21
- 1 Corinthians 13:4-13
- 1 John 4:7-19
- Romans 5:5-11
- Ephesians 2:4-10
- Deuteronomy 7:11-15

Grab your Bible and sit in a comfortable position. Before reading the passage you've selected, ask God to open your mind *and* your heart to what he wants you to learn. Now read the Scripture slowly out loud. Then close your eyes and reflect on what you have read. Notice any words that popped out to you. Ponder these.

Open your eyes and read the passage again, out loud and slowly.

Ask yourself these questions: What does this passage tell me about God? What does this passage tell me about myself? What does this passage have to do with my life? Does anything need to change to improve my understanding or relationship with Christ?

One more time, read the passage slowly and out loud. Then close your eyes and sit in silence with it, listening for any insights that might come through the Holy Spirit.

"Let the word of Christ dwell in you richly, teaching and exhorting one another with all wisdom, singing psalms, hymns, and spiritual songs, all with grace in your hearts to God. And whatever you do in word or deed, do it all in the name of the Lord Jesus, giving thanks to God the Father through him" (Colossians 3:16-17 NET). Your recognition of God's presence in your life will come alive as Scripture comes alive in you. If you persevere, one day, you will realize that the Word of God has become part of your identity.

Chapter 12

The Walk: Stepping Closer to God

So we fix our eyes not on what is seen, but on what is unseen, since what is seen is temporary, but what is unseen is eternal.

—2 Timothy 3:16-17

I would love to tell you that I have the secret sauce for conjuring up God's voice on demand, but that would be a lie. Such a sauce does not exist, and you should beware of anyone who says it does. What I can share with you is that your ability to notice God's presence, recognize God's voice, and discern God's will is possible with practice.

Maturity in Christ and the capacity to grow into a deeper relationship with him takes effort. That effort is not based on hard work in order to earn the right to hear God's voice but rather on your willingness to foster a personal relationship with Jesus so you can discern the Lord's voice when he does speak.

Giving God Control

After years of going through the motions of acting like a Christian (e.g., going to church, saying my morning and evening prayers, and occasionally participating in a Bible study), I recognized that my faith had grown stagnant. I was in a spiritual rut, practicing a rote religion by checking boxes God did not assign.

One day my five-year-old nephew asked me, "Does Jesus live in your heart?"

"Of course!" I answered, but I wasn't sure.

I believed in God, but I did not feel him, and I wanted to feel him. Nothing would change in my relationship with the Lord if I continued doing the same things over and over. God didn't want my religious gestures or my traditions; he wanted my heart. If I was serious about deepening my relationship with Christ, I needed to relinquish control of my life to the One who created it. This sounded scary. If I truly submitted to God's will, what would he ask me to do?

Following Jesus is a choice—a choice that comes with risk. Jesus said, "If any of you wants to be my follower, you must give up your own way, take up your cross, and follow me. If you try to hang on to your life, you will lose it. But if you give up your life for my sake and for the sake of the gospel, you will save it. And what do you benefit if you gain the whole world but lose your soul?" (Mark 8:34-36 NLT).

The question we should all ask ourselves is this: Do I trust Jesus enough to be the Lord of my life?

Money Can Buy Happiness

When a young man asked Jesus how he could obtain eternal life, Jesus told him to keep the commandments.

> "Which ones?" he inquired.
>
> Jesus replied, "'You shall not murder, you shall not commit adultery, you shall not steal, you shall not give false testimony, honor your father and mother,' and 'love your neighbor as yourself.'"
>
> "All these I have kept," the young man said. "What do I still lack?"

> Jesus answered, "If you want to be perfect, go, sell your possessions and give to the poor, and you will have treasure in heaven. Then come, follow me."
>
> When the young man heard this, he went away sad, because he had great wealth.
>
> Then Jesus said to his disciples, "Truly I tell you, it is hard for someone who is rich to enter the kingdom of heaven. Again I tell you, it is easier for a camel to go through the eye of a needle than for someone who is rich to enter the kingdom of God." (Matthew 19:18-24)

Why is it so hard for the rich to enter the kingdom of heaven? The answer has more to do with power than money. As a person's bank account increases, so may his or her sense of self-worth. Self-worth gives rise to pride that leads to control, and control breeds power. As Henry Kissinger, the U.S. Secretary of State during the Cold War, aptly stated, "Power is the ultimate aphrodisiac." The more you have, the more you want.

In addition, power creates envy. The have-nots want what the powerful have, and the powerful hoard what they have in order to maintain control. It is a vicious cycle as the haves and the have-nots jockey for position. Where does God fit in? He doesn't. "No one can serve two masters. Either you will hate the one and love the other, or you will be devoted to the one and despise the other. You cannot serve both God and money" (Matthew 26:24).

If we sincerely want to trust God with our lives, build a personal relationship with him, and easily recognize his voice, we must relinquish control of our resources to the one who provides them. God doesn't ask us to give away our entire bank accounts—though he has every right to—he asks us to tithe. "One-tenth of the produce of the land, whether grain from the fields or fruit from the trees, belongs to the Lord and must be set apart to him as holy" (Leviticus 27:30 NLT).

When I first married Greg, we argued about tithing. Giving away 10 percent of our gross income seemed like too much, and I wasn't willing to start. Greg, on the other hand, had been tithing for years and wasn't willing to stop. My pride and envy, which got in the way of my relationship with both the Lord and Greg, had the potential to do serious damage. "For the love of money is a root of all kinds of evil. Some people, eager for money, have wandered from the faith and pierced themselves with many griefs" (1 Timothy 6:10).

After much soul-searching, I caved. The first step was the hardest, but I've never regretted taking it. Over the years, I've come to discover three things about tithing. First, it keeps envy, pride, and greed in check. Two, God will multiply what you give away just like he multiplied the loaves and fishes. Three, it's quite satisfying to know your money is making a difference. I have personally witnessed how my financial gifts have blessed others, and the joy it brings is indescribable.

"Remember this: Whoever sows sparingly will also reap sparingly, and whoever sows generously will also reap generously. Each of you should give what you have decided in your heart to give, not reluctantly or under compulsion, for God loves a cheerful giver" (2 Corinthians 9:6-7). I have become a cheerful giver. We tithe joyfully and always have enough left over to give away even more.

My heart breaks whenever I hear that another wealthy person has committed suicide. The reasons range from depression to embarrassment and unhappiness to financial difficulties. How I wish someone would have told them how they could have used their money to find happiness and solve their problems—all they had to do was give it away.

Making God a Priority

When we began dating, I couldn't wait for work to end so I could spend quality time with Greg. I loved our Friday night dinners, Saturday morning hikes, and attending church together on Sundays, but the highlight was the conversations. We were never at a loss for words, and laughter was always a given. During the week, we would send each other sweet emails. I compiled many of these into a three-ring binder to remind myself how deeply I am loved.

To this day, Greg and I don't like to be apart for long. Often when I am typing in my office late at night, he will come to join me with his laptop and bring snacks. I can't carry on a conversation with him while I'm writing, but he still prefers to be in my presence rather than alone in another room. Plus, it's nice to have Greg right there where I can bounce ideas off him. To be honest, I am more productive when he is nearby.

Greg calls me every day on the drive home from work. We eat dinner together every night, and then we linger at the table to talk through any plans or concerns. Greg is an excellent listener. We pray together, play together, and never go to bed angry. I cannot imagine life without Greg. He makes me complete.

Before reading on, go back and read the previous three paragraphs again—but this time, read the text out loud and replace "Greg" with "Jesus."

Some of the sentences are not a perfect match, but the point I am trying to make is that the Lord is included in every aspect of my life. Spending quality time with Jesus is not a separate activity on my to-do list that I might never get to. It is a priority. God is at the forefront of my heart and mind, where I can intentionally weave him into every moment.

This wasn't always easy for me to do. But I took my cues from Brother Lawrence, a Carmelite friar who lived in seventeenth-century France and is best remembered for the intimacy he fostered with God. He wrote that the ability to perceive God's presence is available to everyone, provided they abandon themselves completely to God and accept his will for us. This sounded extreme to me when I first read it, but the execution was quite simple. Brother Lawrence said, "that we should establish ourselves in the presence of God by continually talking to Him…"[22]

So, that's what I've trained myself to do. I talk to God when I get up in the morning and throughout the day. He is with me at home, in the car, and anywhere I might go. I ask him to guide my steps. I tell him what I plan to cook for dinner. I request a good parking space at the grocery store. I pull a chair out for him at lunch. I chat with him as I clean. I pray with him when I wake up in the middle of the night. You get the picture. I try to acknowledge God's presence as much as possible 24/7. I'm like a child with my invisible friend.

Because God is my priority and constant companion, I have learned to recognize his presence practically every day. Occasionally, I have the privilege of hearing God's audible voice, but generally, he appears in my surroundings. For example, if my schedule is particularly tight with a writing deadline approaching, a cancelation occurs that I did not instigate. Sometimes God responds to me with visual cues through nature, situations, or signs. When he needs my skills for a specific purpose, I'll get a gut feeling I cannot ignore. God has also sent people into my life with the exact message I needed to hear at the exact time I needed to hear it, but usually, they weren't aware of the role they played in delivering it. Most often, God speaks to me personally through the written word, whether it is through Scripture or the newspaper, or even a secular book. I believe he uses this form of communication to speak to me because I spend a lot of my time reading and writing.

Here's an example of a real-time God-sighting. This morning, I woke early and headed to my prayer chair to begin the day. I began by reading from my favorite devotional book, *Jesus*

ARE Y

Calling. I read, "Save your best striving for seekin[illegible] am constantly communicating with you. To find Me [illegible] voice, you must seek Me above all else. Anything th[illegible] desire more than Me becomes an idol."[23] God knew that I would read this timely text on the very day that I was writing this chapter so I could share it with you as a testament to his active and present presence.

I know that life is busy and full of distractions. But God, the master of time and space, is in the chaos with you. Don't ignore him; include him. Turn to him. Seek him. "Do not worry, saying, 'What shall we eat?' or 'What shall we drink?' or 'What shall we wear?' For the pagans run after all these things, and your heavenly Father knows that you need them. But seek first his kingdom and his righteousness, and all these things will be given to you as well" (Matthew 6:31-33).

There are numerous voices competing for your attention. Turn up the volume on the one voice that matters.

Stay Committed to the Relationship

I don't have a conversion date—the day I suddenly became aware of God. But I do have a commitment date—the day I finally dedicated my life to following Jesus. I had been growing deeper in my faith for several years by reading Scripture faithfully, worshipping weekly, praying daily, and sharing life with a core group of spiritual friends. I thought I was doing well until one day…

While journaling, I felt convicted to confess my sins. It wasn't like I had committed a deplorable crime, nor was I feeling guilty about anything in particular. It was more of an urge to lay down the bricks of remorse I had been carrying since college. These were not new sins, and they were sins I had already confessed, but they were still lingering and felt heavier than usual.

In the privacy of my own home, in the middle of the day, I began confessing my sins again. Suddenly, I was bawling my eyes out, lamenting over all the things I wished I had never done. "If we confess our sins, he is faithful and just and will forgive us our sins and purify us from all unrighteousness. If we claim we have not sinned, we make him out to be a liar and his word is not in us" (1 John 1:9-10). My heart ached as I realized the depth of pain I had inflicted on God's heart through my sins. I was experiencing true repentance.

Falling to my knees, I begged for forgiveness. And then, just like that, it was over. Peace descended as the weight was lifted. Paul wrote in his second letter to the Corinthians, "For sadness as intended by God produces a repentance that leads to salvation, leaving no regret, but worldly sadness brings about death" (2 Corinthians 7:10).

"Who gets the privilege of knowing God? All are invited, but there are established parameters. The door is open for an authentic relationship when we, from the core of our being, make the decision to give our life fully to him."[24] We can study, worship, pray, and fellowship with other Christians, but until we give our hearts fully to God in honesty and obedience, we will remain on the periphery of this divine relationship.

Come to the table with a desire for more of God and a willingness to persevere. Everything you need to develop your spiritual muscles, sharpen your spiritual eyes, and strengthen your spiritual listening skills is already within your grasp. The Bible provides the knowledge of God. Prayer is the communication link to Jesus. Spiritual disciplines open your soul to the Holy Spirit. And Christian community supports and protects the journey.

Do not get discouraged if you don't notice the Lord's presence right away. A relationship with Jesus is a marathon, not a sprint. Remember how long it took before the disciples recognized Jesus as the Messiah, and they were part of his inner circle! It takes time for head knowledge to convert into heart knowledge. So, be patient with yourself, but give it all you've got. A relationship with the King of kings should not be taken lightly. "Commit everything you do to the Lord. Trust him and he will help you" (Psalm 37:5 NLT).

Where from Here?

God wants to be in a relationship with you. He wants to speak to you, guide you, and use you to build his kingdom here on earth. Your relationship with your creator will be personal and unique. Though it will look nothing like mine, we can both take similar steps to get there.

Start small. Pray a little longer than normal or at various times throughout the day. Attend a church service of another denomination. Attempt different spiritual disciplines—go back and work through the GO DEEPER sections of this book. Seek God where you never thought of looking, like the produce section of the grocery store or under your bed. Read the Bible more often. Practice gratitude and generosity. Get to know yourself better. Converse with Jesus more frequently. Repent and repeat. Consistently add a little bit more of God to the mix of your life each day. Through it all, remain attentive and receptive. As you devote more of yourself to your relationship with the Lord, he will strengthen you for whatever is next in your spiritual journey.

When you get lost, which we all do, ask God for direction. He speaks in the language of love and will not rebuke you when you ask for his help. In fact, God wants to bless you with every spiritual gift imaginable in order to transform you "into his image with ever-increasing glory, which comes from the Lord, who is the Spirit" (2 Corinthians 3:18). There is no safer, more joyful, wiser, more loving, hopeful, or amazing place to be than in relationship with God. With an open mind and a willing heart, you will discover that he is more obvious than you ever imagined. Do not allow fear, doubt, indifference, or someone else's opinion to prevent you from cultivating eyes that see and ears that hear God.

Can God speak to you? The answer is yes. Will he speak to you? Maybe.

Are you listening?

Endnotes

[1] Richard Foster, *Celebration of Discipline: The Path to Spiritual Growth* (New York, NY: HarperCollins, 1998 edition), p. 7.

[2] Sarah Young, *Jesus Calling: Enjoying Peace in His Presence* (China: Thomas Nelson, Inc., 2011), p. 179.

[3] Dan Graves, "John Wesley's Heart Strangely Warmed," Christianity.com. https://www.christianity.com/church/church-history/timeline/1701-1800/john-wesleys-heart-strangely-warmed-11630227.html (accessed August 22, 2022).

[4] Michelle Layer Rahal, *Straining Forward: Minh Phuong Towner's Story* (Maitland, FL: Xulon Press, 2018), p. 347.

[5] Shawn Bolz, *Translating God: Hearing God's Voice for Yourself and the World Around You* (Glendale, CA: ICreate Productions, 2015), p. 79.

[6] Jessica Schrader, "Do Dreams Really Mean Anything?" *Psychology Today*, January 19, 2018. https://www.psychologytoday.com/us/blog/supersurvivors/201801/do-dreams-really-mean-anything (accessed June 18, 2021).

[7] Rowan Jacobsen, "Earthly Delights," *Smithsonian Magazine*, June 2021, p. 43.

[8] Adam F. Thompson and Adrian Beale, *God's Prophetic Symbolism in Everyday Life* (Pennsylvania: Destiny Image Publishers, Inc., 2017), p. 83.

[9] C. S. Lewis, *Mere Christianity* (New York: Harper Collins Publishers, Inc., 2001 edition), p. 124.

[10] Mark Batterson, *Whisper: How to Hear the Voice of God* (United States: Multnomah, 2017), p. 162.

[11] John Calvin, *The Institutes of the Christian Religion* (Grand Rapids, MI: Christian Classics Ethereal Library, 1536), p. 44.

[12] Sarah Young, *Jesus Calling: Enjoying Peace in His Presence* (China: Thomas Nelson, Inc., 2011), p. 257.

[13] Mark Batterson, *Whisper: How to Hear the Voice of God* (United States: Multnomah, 2017), p. 97.

[14] David Van Biema, "Mother Teresa's Crisis of Faith," *Time*, August 23, 2007. https://time.com/4126238/mother-teresas-crisis-of-faith/ (accessed August 30, 2022).

[15] Rippon, John. "How Firm a Foundation." *The Presbyterian Hymnal*, 1990, pg. 397.

[16] Francis Collins, *The Language of God* (New York: Free Press, 2007), p. 107.

[17] Dhruv Khullar, "Faith, Science, and Francis Collins" *New Yorker*, April 7, 2022. https://www.newyorker.com/news/persons-of-interest/faith-science-and-francis-collins (accessed December 29, 2022).

[18] Barabara L. Peacock, *Soul Care in African American Practice* (Illinois: Intervarsity Press, 2020), p. 127.

[19] Jon Bloom, "Read the Bible with Your Heart" *Desiring God*, November 11, 2019. https://www.desiringgod.org/articles/read-the-bible-with-your-heart (accessed February 28, 2023).

[20] Dallas Willard, *Hearing God: Developing a Conversational Relationship with God* (Downers Grove, IL: InterVarsity Press, 1984), p. 156.

[21] Timothy Keller, *Prayer: Experiencing Awe and Intimacy with God* (New York: Penguin Group, 2014), p. 146.

[22] Brother Lawrence of the Resurrection, *The Practice of the Presence of God* (New York: Doubleday, 1977), p. 24.

[23] Sarah Young, *Jesus Calling: Enjoying Peace in His Presence* (United States: Thomas Nelson, 2011), p. 71.

[24] John Bevere, *X: Multiply Your God-Given Potential* (United States: Messenger International, 2020), p. 198.

Acknowledgments

When God unexpectedly called me to write my first book, *Straining Forward*, I was sure it would be one and done. But then I began to sense his call to write another book on how God speaks. I did not feel worthy. Who was I to write about God's voice? Even though I had heard it several times and felt the Holy Spirit's presence numerous times, I was no expert. However, I did know enough to pay attention to the signs. As more people started asking when there would be a next book, I surmised that God was telling me that people would read it if I would write it. Therefore, I first want to thank all of you who either expressed interest in reading more of my words or introduced me to people who had God-sighting stories to share.

This book would not exist without those stories. A heartfelt "THANK YOU!" to the following individuals, in order of appearance:

- ♥ Phil, for your illuminating story of God's presence;
- ♥ David and Thomas, for sharing how God speaks to you through dreams;
- ♥ Shontya, for the meaning behind Lira's vision; and Lira, for explaining how visions from God work;
- ♥ Jerry, for sharing your incredible transformation story;
- ♥ Mary Anne, Lori, Melissa, and Jan, for your wisdom on how God directed your lives through doors that either opened or closed;
- ♥ Denise and Megan, for sharing the importance of staying alert to visible signs from God;

- Joan, for attesting to the fact that God still speaks audibly today;
- Curtis and Sheila, for demonstrating the value of listening for God's wisdom in the voice of others; and Gloria, for addressing how God sometimes calls us to be that voice;
- Cait, for providing a big picture view of how God speaks through nature;
- Greg, for tangible evidence of God's control of time; and Tom, for demonstrating the spiritual benefits of relinquishing control of time to God;
- Donna, for sharing how scripture can come alive; and
- Grace, for demonstrating the benefits of relying on God's word for direction.

I gathered many more God-sighting stories from other men and women, but there wasn't space in this book to include them all. As the apostle John wrote, "Jesus did many other things as well. If every one of them were written down, I suppose that even the whole world would not have room for the books that would be written" (John 21:25).

I am beyond grateful to the people who invested their time and wisdom to offer feedback on the flow, the content, and the scripture references I chose to use. Thank you Dalliss Fuhrmann, Denise Ralston, Shontya Washington, Jan Mahumed, Phil Covell, Burt LeJune, and Doug Traxler. You all steered me toward a better outcome.

In the area of scriptural interpretation and application, heartfelt thanks to Reverend Doctor Jonathan Swanson, Reverend Connie Jordan-Haas, and Briane Pittman Kearns. I had wondered if I was overdoing it by asking three theologians for help, but three was the perfect number.

This book would never have made it to print without the loving support of my husband, Greg. God reveals himself to me every day through your encouragement and love.

Finally, and most importantly, thank you Creator God for giving me the privilege of serving you through my writing. All the glory goes to you. May each word I write draw readers closer to you than they ever thought possible.

WHAT DID YOU THINK?

Your review can help other readers find this book.
If you enjoyed reading *Are You Listening?*,
please leave a review on Amazon and/or Goodreads.
If this book inspired you in any way,
please tell others about it, share it with a friend,
recommend it to your library, church, or book club,
or invite Michelle to speak at your next event.

JUST FOR YOU

An additional chapter—this one on how God speaks through physical touch—can be found at:
www.MichelleLayerRahal.com/bonus-chapter.

LET'S STAY IN TOUCH

Website: www.MichelleLayerRahal.com
Facebook: www.Facebook.com/MichelleLayerRahal
Instagram: @MichelleLayerRahal
LinkedIn: www.LinkedIn.com/Michelle-Layer-Rahal

Also, from Michelle Layer Rahal

In the early morning hours of January 31, 1968, New Year fireworks gave way to gunfire and bombs. Eleven-year-old Minh watched in horror as her father and two siblings were gunned down by the Vietcong in their backyard. The tragedy would haunt Minh for the rest of her life and lead her to question God's existence and goodness.

This riveting and true story is told with raw sincerity. It reminds readers that we are all more than victims of circumstance and that even in our loneliest moments, we are never truly alone.

"Michelle Layer Rahal has the voice of a storyteller … a beautiful memoir of survival, self-reflection, and faith."

–Anna Whiston-Donaldson, author of *Rare Bird*

Made in USA - North Chelmsford, MA
26147_9781961732032
11.02.2023 0527